ROSE CAMPBELL

THE
PRINCESS
AND THE PEON

AN UNCOMMON CONVERSATION WITH
THE LATE PRINCESS DIANA

STRATTON
—PRESS—
Publishing Life

Stratton Press Publishing
831 N Tatnall Street Suite M #188,
Wilmington, DE 19801
www.stratton-press.com
1-888-323-7009

ISBN (Paperback): 978-1-64345-504-4
ISBN (Ebook): 978-1-64345-766-6

Printed in the United States of America

FOREWORD

By Marcia McMahon, MA

Rose humorously begins her tale of channeling with a story about a funeral in which she begins to hear the person who is being buried and is lying in the coffin a few short feet from her. Oh, how I can relate to that initial experience! I had this identical experience in my first channeling from a person whom I knew. In this case, it was a former art student who had important messages for her deaf parents. With that surprising event at the funeral, Rose fears she is going crazy. Only later does Rose realize that she has valid information, which might benefit the family of the deceased.

Rose eventually comes to grips with this surprise channeling experience. This event had exposed all of her naivete and self-doubt, which incidentally runs charmingly through this very compelling account of her channeling with Princess Diana. Rose's self-doubt serves to make it a more believable tale that she has indeed heard from Diana, princess of Wales. It is this that sheds much light upon what channeling really is like and how one must accept the spirit realm's contact, regardless of self-doubt. In the second chapter of the book, it is revealed that Diana has connected to Rose upon the first night of her death! Wow! Even I cannot claim to have met Diana so soon in the realms of spirit. What a true honor and testament to Rose's integrity! This only confirms Rose's genuine connection to the late princess of Wales and opens the path for the astounding revelations that follow that first introduction when Rose does not fully believe she is actually speaking to the world-renowned Princess Diana.

Eventually, Rose comes to accept her extraordinary gift from Spirit. I well know the startled feeling, and the feeling of awe, I had when Diana first contacted me! However, in Rose's case, she suspects it is Diana, but it is Diana—the night of her fatal accident—which serves to throw Rose into a state of shock! Rose, being astounded, refers to Diana as **** in these early transcripts instead of using her name, a habit she continues throughout the book.

Rose questions her own spiritual guides heavily about this event. Rose's guides point out a key part of Diana's death and legacy in this statement from them, "It does not matter that she lived only for such a short time span, she will have accomplished more for the gifts of men than if she had lived many, many, years doing only what she could with her physical hands and her physical will" (page 16 of *The Princess and the Peon*).

Now what I found astonishing about their statement is that I am seeing Diana's work through me manifest some eight years henceforth in political messages of peace and diplomacy for the Middle East! Serving as her channel some eight years later, Princess Diana is having an impact on world affairs through my work even today. Diana may be deceased, but her spirit is alive and with us, in fact very much so. I can attest to the truth of that having channeled Diana as I have for four and a half years now and having produced two books with Diana. My first book deals with peace issues in the Middle East into the years 2001–2002. My latest release entitled *With Love from Diana, Queen of Hearts* continues that theme with an emphasis on world affairs from the years 2003–2004 and peace issues in the Middle East. Other topics such as ascension and earth changes are also covered.

Diana, as a growing spirit on that other side, ascended to mastery. Rose's work with Diana documents her ascension process from the standpoint of the newly deceased with concerns about her most recent life to how she rises above those concerns and into the beginnings of wanting to work for world affairs. My work, picking up after this point, shows Diana's compassion and humanitarian endeavor even now. Diana's great works lives on as both an inspiration of her life and charity, but most energetically in her world peace efforts.

Diplomats who knew her in life have read her words; but that is another story.

I was asked recently on the Rochelle Sparrow radio show if I felt that spirit designed it this way; for Diana to die and then do this work through her channels. I said not exactly in that Spirit never designs anyone to die, but that it is true that no one but Princess Diana could do this great work for humanity now! I know that Rose's words from her beloved guides were right on the money some eight years before this work would be manifest from Spirit!

Talk about accurate! Talk about prophecy! Diana still lives among us though her channels, and she even has revealed to both Rose and I that she "shares her crown with her channels." This refers to her crown charka, which is the energy point in the head, or a little above it, when channeling is engaged. IMAGINE this: Rose Campbell wears that crown! While Rose humbly calls herself a peon, she is actually wearing a big bright shining crown, for Diana has symbolically crowned her!

While various notions of royalty are somewhat outdated, it is true that all who read this lovely book by Rose Campbell will revel in the glorious imagery of such thoughts that only Diana could convey such as one chapter called "The Robes of Royalty." Surely Rose could not be making that kind of imagery and eloquence up. One hallmark of Princess Diana that runs through both our works from her is her use of the Queen's English when speaking. There is an eloquence and royal protocol that reveals Diana with a presence of the familiar, yet the sublime, royal lineage of which Diana is most accustomed. Surely Rose, in her role as suburban housewife, would not be comfortable with such imagery!

While reading this book, one is able to connect with many aspects of Princess Diana's thoughts about motherhood and about her beloved sons; her humor about the royals and the truth of the person she intended to be to the millions who mourned her.

Princess Diana's dialogue about her short but very significant life as the modern world's only "fairy-tale princess" sheds much needed light on the truth of her life. It reveals yet again that Diana is indeed working through her channels to bring the truth to light, just as she did in the fine writing of Andrew Morton and his famous book *Diana: Her True Story* while here in this realm. Diana has a purpose in writing through her channels and each is another segment, another chapter of that same person speaking from another realm to our realm. She reveals many fascinating things to her first contacted channel Rose!

Diana speaks now to remove, as it were, the royal title and the tabloid flash to reveal a flesh and bone woman of the world; a powerful magnet for both beauty and goodness that the world so terribly needed. She takes off the crown and gets out of the gilded carriage and speaks on motherhood, on being a part of the servant class whose Cinderella job it was to clean the chambers for the royal household. Diana always speaks in veiled tones about her former family, but her play on words about the toad and the wart that won't come off sent me reeling in laughter the first time I read it! Let it be said here and now that she allows no malice to be said about any royal member of the household, including the newest addition! She said to me recently in a session that she only wishes Charles happiness, so she speaks no other than words of love and light. She is ever at her English best manners, even when utilizing her notorious wit and humor!

It is worth reading through the process Rose encounters within herself in her moments of self-doubt and analytical thinking that make this story one of the most compelling and worthwhile reading experiences I have ever had from another Diana channel! And I know as no other can that this is not the stuff of fairy tales but a true life story of Diana as told to Rose Campbell from one of the world's greatest stars: Princess Diana, whose spirit shines on brightly from her heavenly realms where she continues to work for the good of this realm of form. I can only corroborate this lovely book and its very significant contents as another aspect of that same person I know through my channeling and my work with Princess Diana. I am honored to be working with Rose Campbell, a fine and honest channel. Let us pause a moment in silence for the great gift we have received in being able to hear Diana's voice of compassion and love as it continues to shed her magnificent light!

I cannot recommend *The Princess and the Peon* enough and am assured you will find it very believable if you can only believe in modern-day fairy tales and a deceased princess who speaks to all who will open their hearts and minds to Her!

Marcia's latest book with Diana entitled *With Love from Diana Queen of Hearts* deals with the Middle East conflict and spiritual understanding needed for our world to survive as she spreads her light upon us with diplomatic solutions, which Diana says may save the world further terror!

CONTENTS

Introduction...11

Chapter 1: The Peon Receives an Education..................................15

Chapter 2: The Princess Finds the Peon.....................................19

Chapter 3: The Princess, the Mother, the Land of Make-Believe...29

Chapter 4: The Peon Seeks Answers 41

Chapter 5: The Princess with a Purpose....................................49

Chapter 6: Forms of Tyranny and Love 54

Chapter 7: Destiny, Details, Dying...64

Chapter 8: Memories, Remorse, Conspiracy.................................74

Chapter 9: The Foundation, Fun, and Fergie...............................85

Chapter 10: Mental Movies, Mischief, Merciful Motivations........94

Chapter 11: Soul Choices, Mutual Respect,
Mysterious Symbols 102

Chapter 12: Ironies, Harsh Words, Reformation 109

Chapter 13: Rivalry, Solace, Life's Tapestry................................115

Chapter 14: Emotional Equivalence, Higher Flames, Frivolity ...123

Chapter 15: Working with Others, Continuing Education,
Soul Evolution 134

Chapter 16: Monarchy, Forgiveness, Molding of a King.............139

Chapter 17: Three Convictions 148

Chapter 18: Progress Report, Bitterness of Betrayal,
Foul Weather..162

Chapter 19: Open Forum, New Agenda, Overall Picture
of Creation...174

Chapter 20: Robes of Royalty, Upon the Weaver's Loom............181

Chapter 21: The Peon's Ponderings...190

Chapter 22: The Princess Bids Farewell 200

INTRODUCTION

August 30, 1997, has become one of those dates that bear the distinction of having become burned into the collective consciousness of the world. This date figures prominently in the annals of time as being remembered as a moment within eternity that a bright light and rare beauty became extinguished. The world was left with an empty void that was filled with disbelief and grief. This event affected not only the countries involved but also the world. This one event, this one tragedy, created within the world a response not commonly seen. Individuals, organizations, governments, and entire nations were thrown into mourning. The death of the fairy-tale princess, Diana, Princess of Wales, was an event that unified the poorest of the poor with those of innumerable assets and highest rank. In her death, she was ironically able to create what she had envisioned and was striving to work towards during her life.

The date August 30, 1997 is burned forever into my mind. I imagine that I reacted as most others who were aware of the late-night news flashes about the car wreck in Paris and the death of Diana. However, the wee hours of August 31, 1997, yielded an even larger surprise and more shocking revelation for me than the last hours of the day before. This occurrence astounded me and placed me in a state of doubt, confusion, wonderment, disbelief countered by belief, which was then replaced almost immediately with disbelief again. This mind-bending experience will be covered after I have unveiled some of the mental detours and events leading to it. Knowing about the journey tells you much about where you have arrived.

Realizing that nothing new was forthcoming from the news flashes, I turned the set off. I began thinking about the crash, the people involved in it, and their families. I thought about the pain, both physical and emotional, that this crash had spawned. It was not long until I arrived at the question that I have almost always asked first, ever since I was old enough to verbally form questions—why?

A brief explanation of my belief systems and other related events would shed some light on my thinking processes going into this extraordinary happening and help you as you read this book. I have always believed that most things termed coincidental were not really random happenings. They often seem to have a higher organization behind them than the human beings involved. I have often seen coincidences in my own life, and the lives of others that I know, that proved to be minor miracles. Perhaps not "by the book" religiously certifiable miracles, but something that improved the person's position, mind-set, finances, etc., at a time when needed most. I feel that there are an unlimited number of avenues that something needed may come to you, or unlimited help given, when the mental mind-set of an individual is open to receiving it.

I must also disclose here that I have a sincere belief in many kinds of "helpers" for humankind. I believe not only in what most religions refer to as angels, but also in other spiritual assistants that are not necessarily of angel status. I have for many years spoken to what I call my spirit guides and have received help for others and myself. Their information comes to me verbally; although I do not audibly hear voices. I hear very heavy thoughts that seem to be on a different "wavelength" than my normal thoughts. Through many years of testing the advice and trying to find out if I could stump these "voices," I finally relaxed into knowing that they were real. I also began to make connections for other individuals where my guides would connect me to another person's guides for wisdom and insight for their lives. After almost five years of this type of testing and retesting of the information given and receiving information that I knew I had not known, I have no doubt that all of us have these guides.

One of the many things that the guides helped me to realize is that consciousness does indeed exist after physical death of the body. They explained to me that some of my guides had been human and were now disincarnate. Others of this guidance group had never been human and never would be, but they had a function as well of serving our world with the help of celestial wisdom. I once asked if guides were all "angels," as defined by most religions, and the response was that while angels could serve as guides and protectors, not all guides were angels. Angels may be guides, but some guides could not be angels.

Once I had grown comfortable with the idea of holding a dialogue with someone who was not there (which makes this whole idea sound much more casual than it ever was in reality!), my guides decided to throw me a surprise curveball just to mentally strike me out again. I knew that I could speak to them and to the guides of others for information. This had almost become normal and acceptable to me. Their idea of testing my limits of belief in this process took the form of introducing me to another aspect of speaking to someone who "wasn't there," as most people would define it.

2019 Note:

Ps. Some may wonder why it has taken so long to bring this into a real book form. I had it on a website for years (since about 2003 or so), but there it languished. It wasn't until recently that I had the funds and found a publisher I wanted to work with. I also am no longer raising children, and my husband has died. There is now no one to consider or worry over about fallout or life changes as I had worried about when Diana and I first spoke. As I have grown older, I have felt the press of time upon me, and in part, it is why I do not wish to leave this work sitting on some isolated website or in the innermost vaults of my computer files. I decided that now is the time to give this work a chance at the light of day. Twenty-one years is long enough. I do hope you enjoy this book.

CHAPTER 1

The Peon Receives an Education

In the spring of 1994, I was attending a funeral at a Catholic church for a friend's son. The mass was very interesting to me, having never been familiar with this form of service. As I concentrated on the swinging pots of smoke and the words being spoken, I was brought up short by a thought "voice" in my head asking me to deliver a message to his family and his fiancée. Questioning my own mental capacities, I did what any sane person would do—I ignored it!

Ignoring this aberration on the grounds of possible grief, overactive imagination, too many hypnotic surroundings, etc., seemed logical to me. I can ride in the same saddle with denial for many a long mile if the specter of fear is chasing me. However, when the "voice" kept hailing me, I found it harder and harder to find enough room for denial and I in the same saddle. I eventually had to kick denial off and face the steed of internal fear that was chasing me.

After the pleas were repeated continually, I thought to myself, "What the heck, if I am descending into the realm of absolute and utter madness, go for broke." Thus, I answered the bedeviling voice by asking who it was. I was in such a state of confusion because of what I was experiencing that I had to ask the voice "Who are you?" even though I sit at a funeral and had been asked to give this man's loved ones messages. Actually though, I think I knew who this was and that was the fuel of my fear. I didn't want it to be anybody, much less whom I felt it could be.

What followed after I acknowledged the voice was a half-hour of conversation at the service, which left me shaken and very much confused. I then attended the graveside service and returned to the family's home, unable to fully function. My mind whirled and gyrated around what had happened to me. I also knew that if I relaxed my mental thought processes, this "voice" was waiting to speak to me again. I could feel the presence, so to speak.

During an interaction with some of the family members, I was handed a bombshell that made my stomach lurch like an elevator with a snapped cable. My stomach dropped to my feet, my breath was sucked out of my lungs, and my heart began to do the native war drum rhythm. The family had just mentioned some names and events that I had heard from "the voice"! Reality was beginning to invade my self-pronounced realm of utter and absolute madness.

I had to tell someone about this event, so I shared it with a friend who was with me that day when we arrived back to my home. Her reaction was not what I had feared. She handled it rather well for someone who had just ridden in a car driven by a person who could be delusional. She encouraged me to step forward and take this to the mother of the young man whose funeral I had just attended. I then thought of my friend as delusional!

As the evening progressed, I buried myself in any form of busy work that I could and tried to get denial to hop back into the saddle with me, but I could not do it. The pressure of the presence of "the voice" was with me at every turn. I knew that "it" wanted to speak to me again. About eight o'clock that evening I was so exhausted from fighting my thoughts and the continued mental activity needed to lock out "the voice" that I gave up. I just finally said, "Alright! I give up! If you have something else to tell me, just do it and get it over with." I excused myself to my family pleading a headache (not actually a lie by this point) and retired to my room. There I received more than an hour of conversation with this soul and was so touched that I cried. It had moved from an intellectually weird "something" to an emotionally "something" awesome.

The actual details to this story shall reside with the family, my one friend, and myself. I would not wish to disclose the actual conversation, even if the family was to favor it, because I now feel honored that this young man approached me and shared his thoughts with me. It has become his tribute to me, and mine to him. I did know this young man when he was younger, for he had babysat for my daughter several times. I liked this young man immensely back then, but I now have a much higher regard for him. I did promise him that if I could find a way I would deliver his message to his family.

It took me nine months and an enormous amount of courage to find the avenue to tell his family, but I feel very strongly that he helped me with this also. I had almost decided to forget it and not approach the family, so as not to open any healing wounds. Please remember also that I had no way of knowing if anything he had said to me was true, or if I had indeed imagined all of this. After denial refused to ride with me in the saddle, it seemed that cowardice hopped aboard.

I did take this to the family after events began to happen that I could only view as his pushing me to do so. I am glad that I did because they were able to verify enough from what I could remember of our conversation to help them and to allow me to know that I had shared an incredible experience with this young man. It will go with me to my grave as being the most emotionally touching thing I had ever encountered.

This event awakened a new understanding in me. If I had grown accustomed to speaking to guides who inhabited another realm of existence, why was I so astounded and blown away by the fact that someone real that I had known could also speak to me? To this day, I do not have a good answer to this except to say that when I learned to walk, I had no idea I could run. Running, and talking to deceased people, does not come naturally. It is something that you must learn, sometimes without intending to. As with most things that we must learn, there must be someone willing to teach them to you. As my parents had to allow me to learn to run after they had shown me how to walk, my guides had to allow me this experience as another stepping-stone towards the growth in my abilities.

Eventually, I took this experience and used it as the impetus to learn how to connect others of this world with those of their loved ones who had passed "beyond the veil." The more that I was able to do this and explore the phenomena of receiving information that meant something to those grieving and was indicative of an actual connection to someone in the other realm, the more confirmed my belief system in the existence of consciousness after death became. The education of myself in this ideology was not easily absorbed or taken immediately in stride. There were many years of doubt and testing, and I struggle even now with forms of insecurity. However, the education has been rewarding and highly interesting. I am now thankful for my "chance" encounter with "the voice." It might have been nice though if I could have had at least an introductory class to "Deceased Speaking 101"!

Let us now return to the reason for my asking the particular question: "Why?" My guides, and material from several sources (books, tapes, living people with much esoteric knowledge, not-so-living people with perhaps even more esoteric knowledge, etc.) had informed me that there is a choosing to be born into the world of form and into the general circumstances of that life. Also, at this time of choosing, there is a selection of lessons to learn, to teach, to bring to others through example. Many paths would be presented to us in this life to help us have free will choice of how to do these things, and the choosing itself is entirely free will choice. Most importantly, there is a choosing on a soul or spirit level of how and when to exit the world of form. These thoughts were with me as I asked myself why Diana had left so young. Why now? Why this way? Why when her life seemed to be ready to blossom into another phase that could help so many? I did not have any answers that amounted to anything of importance, so I sought the help of those who had many times before opened the vista of greater truth, higher understanding, and hidden beauty. I asked my guides, and this is the true beginning of our story.

CHAPTER 2

The Princess Finds the Peon

Sitting in the living room of my modest suburban home, I had come face-to-face with a question that I could not find any satisfying answers for. Keeping in mind the abbreviated overview of my belief systems that I provided in the introduction, it seemed only expedient and logical to ask those that I consider to be my spiritual gurus for help with this dilemma.

The process by which I do this is not easy to explain, but very easy for me to accomplish in most environments. The best way I can explain this is that I ask the question aloud in my head and "click" into the right rear of my head to listen in the silence for an answer. As the answer presents itself to me, it is a combination of heavy thoughts and (most times) an ability to almost see the words as if they were scrolling in white letters against a black background. Often there is also a knowing that goes with the words that give more depth of understanding than the words themselves are conveying.

It is possible to also distinguish an emotional tone from the words, even though they are not heard in any auditory way. It was a surprise to me to discover that I could feel someone's anger or their humor. This is not as prevalent with the guides as it is with those who are more newly disincarnate beings. The less time they have been in the spiritual realm, the closer their reactions are to those of us here. It seems that prolonged time "over there" helps to ease, or buffer, the roller coaster of human emotions. This is not to say that they lose all edges of human reaction. Perhaps it just ceases to be so necessary to be relayed. There is great compassion, love, wisdom, humor, and positive feelings abounding with those who have made the adjustment to that realm. It seems the more negative aspects of human feeling dissipates with the passing of time perhaps in part due to learning some of the finer lessons that may not have been gained here in this existence.

I would give you a more scientific explanation of how and why I receive these beings, if I could. I just frankly do not know what physiologically or chemically occurs within my brain for this marvel to happen. I would like someday to have a medical analysis of brain wave activity to see if there is any change during this state, but I am sure insurance does not cover claims for determining "psychic channeling awareness." I have asked for an answer from the higher sources but have been told that I lack the vocabulary and understanding for them to be able to enlighten me upon the changes within my "guidance system" (their words for mind) that allows the connection with the mental and spiritual realms to funnel through my physical apparatus (brain). Imagine how it feels to be told you're not smart enough to comprehend something by someone who isn't there!

The phrasing of my question to my guides about Diana's death went something like this: "Is there a reason, above the obvious one of a car accident, that Princess Diana has left this realm? If so, WHY?" I went into my "reception mode" and was immediately deluged with rapid-fire information. Often there are times when I ask a question of my guides that I only listen and hope I remember what they say. One of the odd points of channeling is that you cannot always remember what comes through, even ten minutes later, if it is a mass of information, something beyond your own knowing, or for another person. There may be a faint recollection of the essence of what was said, but the details or actual phrasing is very hard to recall. This is one of the other reasons that I felt that the information received was not from within me. I felt that if I had made it up, I would have remembered it better.

Due to this glitch in retaining information, I had at one point begun audio recording my sessions. I still do this when pulling through information for other people so that we can play it back if they have questions and they may have a copy to keep. However, rather than going through the hassle of recording and then transcribing information for myself, I taught myself to receive and type at the same time. Mind you, the reading can be rough, and the words spelled backwards, but the spell checker and grammar features of my computer have saved the day!

When the guides burst through that evening with more information than I knew I was going to be able to handle easily about their reasoning for her death, I excused myself and moved to my computer. In hindsight, if I had not, I would to this day be kicking myself. What I received opened my eyes wide and has changed many perceptions and feelings within me. If I had not recorded what I received, word for word, I could never have accurately remembered the potency of the words or have had an ongoing record of a most monumental event. Not to be melodramatic, but part of modern-day history would have been lost in the cobwebs of my gray matter.

I moved to my computer at about 1:30 a.m. (EST) on August 31, 1997. I knew enough about my channeling abilities to know that I would not remember well what they were going to say to me the next day, especially since I was already so tired due to the lateness of the hour. When they started speaking, and it became evident that I wanted to remember what they were saying, I turned on my computer and asked the question again.

What will follow here is a verbatim transcript of what I received. This is done for two reasons. I could sum up what was said, but you would not get to experience the flavor of the actual words, and I don't think I could put it as succinctly in my own words. Also, this book isn't about what I think, except for random comments and setting the stage, but rather a presentation of the actual conversations that I experienced. I may not quote all of it verbatim, but I will be very careful to follow the true meaning of what was said. Since their phraseology is different than ours sometimes, I will add clarifying remarks in parenthesis. My words are denoted with the symbol *R.*, the guides with the symbol *G.*, and other "speakers" are designated with either an initial or the symbol ****. (All of Diana's words are preceded by the **** symbols). If I am unsure of their identity or wish to keep the identity hidden to casual prying eyes, I use this latter symbol.

Let us begin now the true purpose of this book. Be prepared for some new views and uncommon conversation.

> R. "After receiving the news about Princess Diana's death, what would you say about the reason for it? Is there a meaning here that is above the obvious?"
>
> G. "There will always be the meaning assigned to these events that are ascribed to those thoughts associated with the world of physical (human life). There is also however that which is of the world of spiritual to be considered, and we will give to you the words of our world upon the events that are perceived by your world. There are concepts within your world that are of no value to the world that is of no physical form (spirit world). There is the concept of being well guided with only the wisdom from within your own guidance systems (minds), and then there is the concept that when events are happening there must be given to it only that which can be seen or explained. It is also given that there is a conceptual format that if there is a good then there must be an evil, if there is a will there is a roadblock, and if there is life then there must be a death. It is this that gives your world the greatest difficulty when dealing with the view that when someone dies then there will be no more good accomplished through that person. It is our world's wisdom that when one is of the world of physical there can only be given the good that

can be accomplished within the scope of that person's realm of influence. There can be, however, greater influence given when one resides within the world of the spiritual realm and can therefore affect many more through their death than through their life. It will be shown that when she was what your world calls alive she accomplished many things that were of great benefit and need for those of your realm. It will also become evident that through her death many more things will be accomplished in her name than would have ever been possible for her to orchestrate while having only the influence of her physical life. She will become even greater in her scope to help others through her death than through her life within the physical environment. The concept that what one does, and can do, will end with the death of an individual is a concept that has no meaning for our world. It is a given that when one leaves the world of physical for the world of spiritual their power of influence has been magnified many times over. It is not given to our understanding that when one leaves the earth plane that their work or wisdom is no longer within existence. It is her will to be given the benefit of her life to accomplish much through her death and this will be self-evident within a very short time, as your world knows it.

"There is always a reason that someone chooses to leave their physical bodies and continue their work and their lessons. It was not her choice to live within the world as she was living, but to make the transition into the spiritual realm to make a bigger difference to those whom she wished to help. Think about the effect that her death will have upon the world as they reflect upon those issues that she was working upon when she left your world. There will be many who will be given the urge to pick up the gifts she had given and make them even more focused upon the issues because she is now gone. There will be those who will make a larger effort to make them become realities to honor the one who led the way. It will increase in scope and depth because she is no longer among your world and this will begin that which can change many things that she herself could not do. It will now become a given within your world for the good that she tried to do to be given the energy of many to make them feel better with her passing. It will now be the things she did that will become the battle cries of the masses and she will have made more impact through her death than through her life. There will be many more who are of wanting to make her a national symbol for the downtrodden and she will achieve a fame for the good works that she was of making her own than she would have had she lived many more of your earth years.

"It is not that she is dead and gone, but that she is dead and giving to others that which she cared for deeply. It will be the beginning of a reformation within her country to make her the one whom was of greatest concern for the well-being of the masses and lead them to see that she was not only their princess, but also their way-shower. She will make them see through her death more than they could ever see within her life. It is her spirit that will live on through these works and this is the concept that we are of wanting you to see. It does not matter that she lived only for such a short time span, she will have accomplished

more for the gifts of men than if she had lived
many, many, years doing only what she could
with her physical hands and her physical will."

How prophetic these words to me were! Everything mentioned
to me within a short time of her death has been brought about or
came to light. There has been a movement mounted to make her a
symbol for the downtrodden. Her memorial fund has begun to aid
many and, as more monies are received, will continue to do so. Her
death has caused many to reevaluate their own forms of giving and
working for those less privileged. She has become more famous in
her death as regards her humanitarian efforts than she was in her life.

Having also lost another great humanitarian (Sister Theresa)
within the week of Diana's death, I could not help but compare the
difference of their leaving this world with their contributions to it. It
seems that Diana's death has inspired more people to greater works
and a higher expression of themselves than Sister Theresa, even
though Sister Theresa devoted more than a half a century to this
cause. Once again it would seem that the guides were correct. Diana's
death had inspired more good works than another's prolonged life
had done. When I asked my question of why Diana had left, none of
these reasons had occurred to me, but as the guides spoke I felt the
truth of their words. As the months sped by after her death, I began
to see the depth of the truth they had spoken to me about the reasons
for her death.

Again, we shall return to a verbatim account of what transpired
this night. More information that I had never thought about was
given to me. I once again was loaded aboard an emotional roller
coaster.

G. "There is someone who wishes to speak
to you, and we are of wanting you to make the
effort to make this contact. Think about allowing us to connect you with this other and allow
them to be your guide on why this tragedy will
make the gifts that Diana had so well given to

the world of man. Our world is ready to make the connection if you are of giving us the consent that we seek."

R. "I will give you this consent, but please make it short and concise. I am tired and cannot go on for much longer."

G. "We are now ready and ask that you give your will to our fellow worker of spirit."

R. "Yes, go ahead. I am listening."

**** "It is not that I am able to make you give me your will, but will you allow me to speak freely with you for the purpose of making you know that I am who I say that I am?"

R. "Sure. Go ahead. I will allow you to say what you wish but can't guarantee that I'll believe it or understand it all. Fair enough?"

**** "I will not give you my real name, but I can give you this: I was not allowed to make the world see that I was able to give them more of the same as they had given me and I think I was killed for this reason. I was a good way-shower in my own fashion, but there was much dispute about who I really was. It wasn't that people misunderstood me; it was that there was not much that anyone could do with the will of the masses to know that I was not the person that they wanted instead of the person that I was. I was handed the gift of being made famous, but it was not that which I readily sought. I was the given the gift of being most guided to be made into someone that I was not and this was a gift that I was trying to return to the world. I was not given the chance to know that I could make myself the most misunderstood person by simply being me and that I gave the world what it was looking for without understanding that I was losing me in the process. I was not given the choice to become what I had envisioned; I had to become what others envisioned. I was only making myself more of whom they wanted until the day I realized that I was no longer there within my own shadow, but only a cardboard character that had painted on a smile and a persona. I was not really living my life for me, but for those who did not really know me. It was not the way that I wanted to live and therefore I tried to give up on life. Even in this I was not allowed to do as I wished and this makes me sad to realize that when one becomes an icon, one cannot simply choose to become one's self again. It is not that I am without wisdom that what one wants and what one gets is a fight that many must undergo. It is that I am able to say, with a fair amount of certainty, that what one wants and what one is given may be so far from the beginning so as to be unrecognizable. I think if I had the chance to make the choice again, I would have learned sooner to be real to myself and allow no one the control to shape my life other than the one living it."

Having advanced my education since the time I had spoken with the young man at his funeral, I was at least smart enough to have an extremely creepy feeling about who the speaker of this missive could be. I am not saying that at this time I believed fully that I was speaking to HER, but the words that I was receiving were causing me to go into one of my "grab denial and put it in the saddle again" modes. I realized that at this point the words could probably apply to many people who had passed over. Still a nagging feeling was pressing down upon me, and I wanted to deny what my heart knew with the cool, clear logic of my mind. I can say that at this point I was no longer tired and thinking of sleep! The adrenaline was pumping and curiosity was raging. I was thinking while I was listening and typing. (This is what I meant about a different "wavelength" than my own thoughts. I can hear myself thinking other thoughts while being "addressed" by the other person.) I am mentally arguing with myself that this can't be who I am feeling it might be. I was asking myself, "If it is, how could she, and why would she, want to communicate so soon after she had died?" The biggest question of all, of course, was, "Why to me?" As I bounced these ideas around in my mind, my heart was already knowing and responding. I was feeling sad for this person, whomever it might be. I felt their despondency and their resignation to events that were beyond their control. I could detect a latent anger that was not explosive, but definitely there. I could feel a wanting to unburden and a wanting to have someone know what he or she was feeling. My mind was not ready to accept, but my heart knew. Soon enough though, my head had to shut up and let my heart lead.

I should add here that much of what you shall be reading soon are her views as stated to me at this particular time. There were over 120 pages of transcripts delivered to me conversationally in increments spanning a year. Her ideas and views did evolve as the time passed. You will see the shift in the focus of what she says she wants to accomplish and her earlier feelings changing as she gains either more wisdom or emotional distance. The next segment of the first transcript follows, and you will see for yourselves why my heart finally won out over my logic.

CHAPTER 3

The Princess, the Mother,
the Land of Make-Believe

This first transcript is broken up into parts to present it in the best order of her disclosure to me. It is a lengthy volume of thoughts and emotions to handle in one dose, so bear with me as we travel through this first session. As I have said before, not all of the material may be presented in verbatim form, but I felt it important for this first encounter with her be delivered to you as it was delivered to me. I wanted you to experience the power of her words, to see why by the end of this session I had very little doubt about the speaker, and to judge for yourselves if my heart was wrong to silence my attempts at logic. In later sessions, I was given enough information that would prove to my intellect that my heart had been correct. Even if not all of the information was verifiable, or I had received some ideas inaccurately, there was enough advanced knowledge of certain events that my intellect and the intellect of those I had shared this secret with had been satisfied. Now...back to the conversation.

> **** "It is an awful experience to live your life as an outside observer and think only with the thoughts that are preprogrammed by others. It is not that there is wisdom in giving others

no control of your life, but that to give all control over to another is a form of self-mutilation. I feel as if I had been given the choice between living without feeling alive, being alive without living, or feeling that there was no way to make either choice without being dead to who I was. It was not a good life as I was concerned, and I feel more alive now than I have since the rebirth of my soul into the body that I left. I think that should I ever choose to come back into the world of being alive, then I will choose to do so far more carefully.

"I think that you know that I am who you are afraid that I might be. I am sorry that you have to make the choice to use this or make it another part of the sad history that gets buried with the image that will go into the ground with me. I am not going to make this a gift to you alone, so make no mistake that I have expectations of any sort for you. I have given up all control of making the world happy and I think that you should use this only as you see fit. It will not make me anything if you should make the choice to burn or destroy this bit of sentimental rubbish, just as it will neither make me any more if you give it to those who would make themselves happy to have my final thoughts about that which was called my life. It was with a good bit of irony that I used with that statement if you are unable to make out the tone of my final words. Thank you for making me happy that there is another way to deal with this gift of communicating with others. I think that I can make the world feel my presence within my newest kingdom."

I found it interesting that she brought to my attention that what I did with this unique encounter would have little ability to affect her one way or the other in her new abode. Upon reflection of this statement, I understood the truth of these words. Also, just because I thought I "heard" that she was who I feared she was, I still did not blindly accept. After all, if I were making this up, wouldn't I say something like that to myself? It was the following words that struck the cord in my heart, and I knew that I had never entertained any such thoughts as she shared with me next.

> **** "It wasn't the fairy-tale princess's life that I led, it was the life of the one who got left behind to make the beds and cleanse the chamber pots so that the house would look good if anyone came to visit. The window dressing was fun, but it was so unnecessary to make me happy. I was wanting the fairy-tale princess's life, but what I got was the ugly toad and the wart that wouldn't come off. I am regretful that my children will be within much sorrow for me, but then again, I was only the instrument that kept them alive until they grew into the heirs of the kingdom of the toad. I was not able to give them what they needed, which was a mother who could help them be who they wanted to be, and this was a deep source of pain for me. I was the only one who could make them see that when one grows up in a fairy tale then one can only hope to be the prince or the pauper. It wasn't the way that it had to be, but then it was not a way that was going to change simply because I woke up from the dream and wanted to leave the kingdom. It was only going to go from bad to worse if I had made them see that they had choices for their life because I knew down deep that there was no way they could escape the fairy tale, based on who

they were. I had created them to be whom they were born to be and I couldn't begin to make them not become the next prince and the next king within the kingdom. It was not a way that I could control for them and I felt sorry that they had been born with no choice for their lives. I am regretfully a very sorry mother if I cannot allow my children the freedom to choose their life's course and this is an understanding that came too late. I was living the fairy tale when I conceived and I was living the fairy tale when I gave birth to them. I am now no longer living the fairy tale and I now know that I had no right to make them come into the world of being who everyone else thought they should be. It was a source of pain for me to have to say that I made a mistake by giving my children their lives, but that is how I had come to feel.

"I cannot change their destiny and that made me angry and sad that they have so little choice over whom they are to become. I made the mistake of having them, but I do not wish to make the mistake of giving them the feelings that they need to be someone else when they will have no choice in the matter. It is not by choice that one lives within the kingdom of the toad, it is by birth. I have done much to establish for them the thought that they can become even greater men than their forefathers, and this is the best that I could do for their lives. It is not for them that I left my world of being the fairy-tale princess, but for myself. I am afraid that my leaving the kingdom made little difference for them in the final outcome of their lives, except to show them that there is another way to have them believe in themselves. They know now that when one is a prince or a princess that there is very little choice of what one must become, except by leaving the kingdom some and making the fairy tale seem less real. It will serve them well, I believe, when they are able to make their own way within the world of being princes, and when the day comes that they must become king they will know that if they so choose they can make the fairy tale good and kind and believable. It is this that I have left them and I pray that it will be enough to help them see that I meant them no harm by making them to be princes. I, too, was living the fairy tale and had to make my choice on how I would make the fairy tale believable for me. I am deeply regretful that I could no longer live the fairy-tale life, but I have shown them the power of make-believe versus the power of real life and real living. May that be given to me as a credit for having made them for their father and their country."

Powerful, isn't it? As a mother myself, I found myself sitting there with tears flowing freely down my face. I do not cry easily. This is when I KNEW I was not making this up. I had never had my thoughts drift into this region of understanding. It was so far removed from anything I had ever thought about. I was never a royal watcher, and except for limited news blips that I caught here or there, I didn't think much about the royal family. I happen to be one of those Americans who pays little attention to what goes on in our own power structure, much less one that is thousands of miles away with minimal effect to my personal world. I have enough to handle with working, household duties, coordinating schedules for six of us, helping those I know personally, and using my "strange" abilities for others in my spare time. If I had ever given the heirs to the throne any thought, it was more along the lines of how lucky they were. Having a grandmother who was queen, a father who was next in line, a beautiful and loving mother, personal servants, private schools, never having to wear secondhand clothes, going on ski trips and yachting adventures, riding horses, etc. It seemed like a pretty good deal to me compared to my life of stretching dollars, never having been more than 500 miles from home, washing my own clothes and those of five others, etc. I have to be honest here and say I did not have many sympathetic thoughts concerning their plight!

Her words to me awoke me from my own stupor of not thinking about the royal family. Yes, maybe my children do not have the materialistic advantages of the princes, but they do have the potential to choose whatever they may do with their lives. I have the satisfaction of knowing that even if they must work to put themselves through college, they made that decision. If they choose to not get a higher education and become a minimum wage worker, that was their choice also. They can choose to marry, have children, stay celibate, change religions, proclaim atheism, live in a hut in the woods, or make any multitude of choices. Being an American, the right to choose is so ingrained in me that her words struck me with full force. Neither our whole country nor an established hierarchy could limit their choices as to what their lives would become.

This confession of a mother's concern about this matter was very real to me. As I have said before, I could psychically feel her emotions. They were not a raw as my own because she has had more time to contemplate them, but they were there. As a mother, I felt incredible sorrow for her. I would also have a difficult time accepting that everyone else was choosing my children's destiny. Can those of you who are parents say you feel differently? Perhaps you can, but for me this was a tragically sorrowful revelation. I am not saying that I feel sorry for the boys, they may be extremely happy with their lot. My grief here was for the person, the mother, that I spoke with in the silence of my office. Later in our conversations, she offered me a different understanding that she had gained about this issue, and this will be presented in due time. It made me feel better for her.

One of the reasons that I have chosen to come forward with my experience with Diana is because I was given a copy of Andrew Morton's commemorative edition of *Diana: Her True Story*. A friend, knowing of my experience, brought me a copy of this book less than a month ago when she came to my home. I picked this up as casual reading one evening and went into a marathon reading session. Many things in this book (which I did not read until August 1998) echoed the information that I had stored in my computer. In particular, dealing with what we have just discussed, his chapter entitled "I Did My Best" supported much of what she said that first night with me. Page 206, second paragraph, choked me up again with the flashback of emotion that I had experienced when I first heard of her regrets about her children's lack of choice. For those of you who do not have the book, I shall quote this short paragraph:

> William and Harry were aware of their destiny. On one occasion the boys were discussing their futures with Diana. "When I grow up I want to be a policeman and look after you, Mummy," said William lovingly. Quick as a flash Harry replied, with a note of triumph in his voice, "Oh no you can't, you've got to be king." (Morton, 1992)

How easy it was to understand her statements to me after the reading of this incident. I am sure this may have caused any caring parent despair.

One other quick comment: I am sure that her reference to "what I got was the ugly toad and the wart that wouldn't come off" will cause many a raised eyebrow and consternation in some circles. However, this tickled me. At a different point in time, I had asked her why she had chosen the analogy of a toad rather than the usual one of a frog. (You know, kiss a frog and get a prince?) Her answer to me was insightful and humorous also. Having not recorded it, I will deliver it in summary. Whereas a frog chooses to live in an environment that is fluid, close, soothing, and people choose them as pets to love, a toad chooses conditions that are harsher, dry, surface-oriented, and there are fewer who would choose to hold them close. Her words on this gave me a new understanding to the use of this analogy. The significance of "the "wart"? She asked me to reach my own conclusion to her meaning. I have finally done so but will allow you the same privilege.

Let us move forward with the last and final part of this first transcript. After this is finished, I shall move through most of the other material using excerpts of the message so as to speed us along. However, rest assured that I shall cover all that is important and use her words where none other would suffice.

> **** "I am now growing tired of being here (in this conversation?) and I will make this gift to you. I am not going to reveal my name, but this will be no hindrance to you should you choose to make this my final words. I am also sure that you know that there is no money that will be made through my words that can give you satisfaction, so you must choose carefully if you are to make the right choice. It is of no import to me what becomes of these words for many will believe them, and many will not. I feel those who knew the real me will recognize the value of what was said here, but for the average person they will only gaze upon them and feel pity that I have died and am no longer the fairy-tale princess.

> "What is of most importance for me now is to know that I am now able to make the headlines and the tabloids make someone else their fairy-tale princess and I can be who I have always been. I wasn't given the choice before, but now I can continue with my true work and make the world feel their own guilt at having poverty and war within their kingdoms and making the princes and princesses more important to the story than the paupers. There is no one more important than the paupers for they are the kingdom. It was a concept that I grew to understand during my reign as the fairy-tale princess who was only

a pauper that made the mistake of kissing the toad. All will know, because of my life, that not all lived happily ever after in the kingdom of the toad. It will do well as a message that I was able to convey that not all fairy tales have happy endings and that not all fairy tales should be handed down to those who come after. I am hoping to see the gift that my children possess to make their choices to live in the fairy tale, but not in the land of make-believe. To be a prince or princess is to live in the fairy tale, but that does not mean that one must live in the land of make-believe where there are no mistakes, no desires, no urges, and therefore no humanity. I was living proof that to make-believe is to make a mockery of the fairy tale. There is no castle that has no dragon, and if you pretend that it doesn't, then you live in the land of make-believe."

R. "I love your analogies. I feel great compassion for you and I feel that you are a woman who always knew who you were somewhere inside of you or you would never have known and awakened to the fact that you were living nothing more than a fairy tale. It would have become real for you and you would still be the princess sitting in her ivory tower. I don't think I will share these words with the world at large for now, because I feel that the whole world pried into your life and I don't think it fair that they pry into your death. If you feel I should, let me know, and if I change my mind I'll let you know. What do you say?"

**** "I am not given to wanting them to know that I am able to communicate with anyone just yet, so please give this some time before we make this decision. I am not going to make you the one to choose, but I ask that you not be the only one to choose. I will make my wishes known with this later. Thank you for your kindness of making me feel able to make a connection and I think you had better keep this to yourself for the time that we are not communicating with each other. I will give you my answer on this later, after I have spoken to another who will make this matter clearer. I am your friend and you are my friend for we have been more honest with our feelings than I had been with most whom knew me in life. I will return to you and give you my formula for the good life that a fairy-tale princess can live if she doesn't get lost in the land of make-believe. That will be our next discussion and then we can decide if we want to make this a public format. Thank you as well for your kindness and your wisdom about being that sure of myself. Perhaps you are right. I always did know that I was living in the land of make-believe, and I forgot that I was a pauper in a princess's dress. Until then, I will remember you fondly and I ask that you not make me sad for having left by being sad for me. I never could stand pity and I think that you are a very wise person to know that I am not grieving for what I left behind. There is no ache worse than the one I had while I was alive and that is now eased. I have only the regret of leaving my children behind to make me feel like sadness even exists here in this realm, but for the most part, the sadness here is just an echo of the sadness I knew alive. Good night and good day."

Sleep was nonexistent for me that night. My mind raced trying to rationalize what my heart had told me. I had very little doubt that I had made this up by the time I had turned my computer off, but still, being the logic-driven person that I am, I had to integrate the concept that this was possible. I am not talking about the concept that there is communication between "our" world and "their" world. I had already spent many years testing this and was personally satisfied that actual communication had occurred, especially as the families of the ones who spoke to me verified some pretty specific information. My source of uneasiness this day was the fact that the princess had spoken to such an unknown peon as myself. (Hence, the reason for the title of this book!) I had no doubt that she would be able to communicate if she and the world of spirit so chose. I had no doubt that what I had witnessed was not me being creative so late in the evening. I had no doubt that the ideas I had received could be fitting for her. My question to myself over and over, as is usual for me, was why?

Why me? Why not someone who was a famous medium? Why so quickly? Why at all? Why these statements? On and on it went. I had no answers. I had only a knowing deep inside of me that this was real. I had a knowing that if I never spoke to her again, it would do nothing to negate what I felt then. I knew also that I was standing on something that threatened to throw me overboard into some very choppy mental waters. I needed to learn to swim quickly but did not know where to find a teacher.

I honored her first statement to me and shared this with only my husband, for a short time. I felt my husband had a right to decide for himself if I had gone over the edge. His remark to me was "Why you?" Thankfully though he did not look up the number of any psychiatrist that could see me immediately! But there was that damnable question again! However, his next response made sense. He suggested that if it had been her, and she had said we would speak again, to wait and see what happened. What clarity an objective person can give you! I had been feeling like I needed answers NOW! His remark opened a new avenue of relief for the mental anguish that I was under. Sure, why not wait to see what was next? That put the ball in her court, so to speak. If I never received anything else, then I could keep the file in my computer and someday look back at it and maybe even laugh. If I had no more conversation with her, then I didn't have to do anything. Just chalk it up to some weird and unexplainable event, some undefined mental glitch and get on with the housework. The mental relief this gave me allowed me to sleep like a "dead person" that night. (Pun intended!)

One of the things that many people who know me will attest to is that I have the inability to know when to quit analyzing, when to give up on an issue, when to leave well enough alone. So, true to my character, I was unable to go very long before I had to at least speak to my gurus, both physical and spiritual, to get their insight. My three friends who know most of my work, and whom I consider not only reliable but also part of my mental health/reality measurement system, took this in stride. They had enough belief in my abilities and me to almost be blasé about the whole thing. A combined response was something like, "Yeah, so? Why not you?" Reassuring, but not hard-and-fast answers. I then turned to my spiritual gurus to see what they had to say. This, it turned out, reopened the can of worms I had tried to seal shut. You know, some people just don't learn very well unless you thump them on the head over and over again. However, if someone hadn't been stupidly curious, many things in this world would never have been found, invented, realized, or changed. Yes, stupid curiosity has given us many great things, and perhaps these words I am sharing with you will prove to be another example.

CHAPTER 4

The Peon Seeks Answers

On the evening of September 2, 1997, I sat once again at my computer and asked my guides to speak to me about the visitor that I had spoken to. I asked them for understanding on this and what the purpose of this conversation had been. I was actually hoping that they would tell me that it had been some form of test, some sort of practical joke on their part, or that they would admonish me for making up the words in my head. No such comfort was offered from the world of spirit. Their response to me will be offered to you in segments. I will condense and select the key points, as my guides can be long-winded on even the simplest of questions, and they had much to say on this subject.

> G. "It was a gift to you to make you aware that you can and do have the power to make the wisdom of all of our world available to the world of physical and we were given the chance to make this connection to you with her will of wanting to make another gift to the world of her most given thoughts upon her life....It is of great value that you are able to receive her with the clarity that you do and we are of wanting you to make the gift to her to work with her for the giving

of the world her good and loving spirit. Our world will make her the gift that is always giving through those like yourself and she will lead many to see that her life was not one of wanting to be the golden Princess, but the gifted Queen of compassion....It is her gift to the world to have chosen to make herself an example of great compassion and great ability to make the wisdom of the masses begin to realize that if one can work for the betterment of those below them, then all will be elevated."

I was getting the feeling that they were hinting that I should go public with this conversation, yet I had reservations. Reservations, not only because I had promised her to not do so, but because I was not at the belief comfort zone where I wanted to run out and proclaim any such thing to the world. I asked them about this.

G. "It is our intent to make you see that you have the gift of doing so, but that it is your own will that will make the choice. Give this some thought and think also about the fact that she is of wanting to make you her given wisdom giver for the furthering of her work...It is not that you must do these things, it is that you have the choice to do these things."

I didn't understand then that they had more knowledge of what was being set up than I could have begun to guess at. I wasn't going to just run out and do anything because they said I could if I chose to. I felt this definitely was not something I wanted to do. I had, as of yet, not had any more contact with Diana; and at that moment, I felt it foolish to even consider going public.

I'll bet you can't guess what my next question to them was. Okay, you are right. It was, WHY ME? One of my three friends had offered the theory that perhaps Diana had sent her thoughts out to the world in general and many who have gifts similar to mine had received them. I liked this idea immensely because it took the strain off me. One of the reasons it has taken me almost a year to make a decision as to what to do with this vast amount of information is that I have been waiting for something to come forth from others who had been brave enough to state publicly that they had spoken to Diana. Perhaps someone has, but I am yet not aware of it. If I were, it would make this entire project less scary for me. I summed up this theory for my guides and asked them if this was indeed the case.

> G. "It is given to you and to others, but it is you who can become a gifted channel for her, if you so choose. There is no given pressure for you, it is the will of her to use you, but then again if you choose not to do this then there will always be another that may give this unto the world. It is your choice and we are only suggesting that you make this assignment a gift to yourself....It is our wish that you speak to her again and allow her to make the gift to you of presenting her wishes to you and this will be the given time for you to make your decision. It is not of our wish that you give her your answer unless you have given this several gifts of thought...make your will known to her only after you have considered this with much depth. It will make you the gift of being well-known and this is of great benefit and great hindrance.... Allow her now to speak to you and make her work at convincing you why she has given us to understand that she has chosen you to be her spokeswoman....It is our gift to be of your service and we make this our work with great pride and great wisdom that you are of the ability to do that which you choose."

Their formal and stuffy speech patterns are one reason I had begun to figure out that their "voice" was different than my own thoughts. I tend to use slang, contractions, exclamations, and language shortcuts. Obviously, they don't. They also seem to try and see how long an answer they can give me to any question when I would prefer just a simple yes or no answer. I have to sit through a monologue each time!

I did allow a connection to Diana that evening. What happened was a question and answer session. Again, I will try to short-cut through the material and yet not lose the true essence of the conversation.

R. "Why are you so interested in this world's affairs when you are free of them and could forget them?"

**** "I am never free of the world that you live in and neither shall you be. It is not as if you leave there and arrive here with no thought of those you have loved and those who would still benefit from who you are....What I need from you is the chance to make my final words mean something to that world and help the world that loved me see how wrong they were to make me the princess that no one could be. I was well aware of the world's opinion of me, and yet they never really knew what I was like and how I felt inside. I was given over to great bouts of depression for what I saw of the waste and extravagance and cavalier way of taking so much for granted in the royal life. It was not that I did not make these things available to myself, you understand, and I am well aware of the hypocrisy that I am guilty of also. I was not able to withstand the mentality of being the one who had the right to all that I chose, and I never gave myself over to the worldview that I was any better than the common man. I was made, to a great extent, to utilize the resources at my disposal and this does not make it right either. I had a view that all who were in poverty should be given a start out of the royal coffers which would go a long way in making the level of poverty within the country more equitable to those who had great wealth. This was not a view that was given to the ones who had the wealth with any effect.

"I was young and naive to think that one could simply choose to share what one had if that be their wish. It was a view that gained me much reproach for having spoken of it and I am glad that I can now say these things.....I was never well liked within the confines of the family for I was far too eager to make a difference for the ones who had no power. I was ridiculed many times for siding with the wrong source, the wrong agenda, the wrong way of being. I was never happy after I moved into the palace and I was only trying to make the world a better place and a place that I could call my country. I was not allowed to make the world as I saw it to be, I had to make myself the way they wanted me to be seen. It was a great deal of stress for me to attend functions for the under-privileged knowing that I wore more and ate more than could ever be given to those whom we claimed to be helping.....I became aware that to make the world love the ones who needed it, I had the power to do this precisely because I was of the royal family. If I could not make a difference with the wealth, then I would make the difference with the power that the royal family accorded me by being who they thought me to be. I was able to make many people see through my eyes that there were great issues of injustice and need and for this I am grateful that I became the fairy-tale princess. It was not all that I hoped to accomplish, but it was far more than I could have ever done as the Diana that had been a Lady without the royal family and royal title to make the forum so wide spread....I will make the gifts posthumously through the same means that I used while alive. I will make the gifts given to me by the royal family work even beyond what they could have foreseen, and this will be of benefit for the world they rule and their world of power-lessness to control. I am going to make this a gift to them also, for when they realize that I can and still do feel for the common man, they may realize that they need to look further beyond what they have accomplished for their own gain and works of power to the gifts that they will have to make when they are no longer the royals of Britain, but the common man of this world of spirit....It may catch on with the ones who have the power to make the change within the country and the world so that there will be a giving spirit for those who would be king.

"I am now wanting to ask you if you are wanting to make the pledge to give me the gift of your abilities and if we may work together for the benefit of many. I am well aware that you are of no mind to make the world work for their wisdom and that you want to make a difference within your own world as well, and I say that we may accomplish both. It would not be only for my benefit or the benefit of my causes that this could be a successful union, but for the whole world who believes that I have spoken through you. It is a given that there will always be those who do not believe and this you must consider for it is you that will be there within the world to take the brunt of their cynicism. I have no gain that can give me satisfaction if I cause you undue stress and this is unfortunately the thing that may make you or another reluctant to be my spokesperson. I am well aware of the way that you may be received within the world and I ask that you give me your opinions based upon this. Are we of understanding that I am not going to make you the spokesperson if you cannot be committed to the process even if the going is of great difficulty within the first few given sessions that we give to the public? Remember well that I have been there on the front pages and on the front line of fire. Remember well also that I was unhappy with this until I learned to make it work for me instead of against me....make no mistake that it is you who will have to have the inner strength that it takes to survive. I am no more able to make the difference with the media than I did while living within your realm....I will give you some time to make the decision, but I am eager to make myself known while the gifts that are being given are still of being under control of those who will make certain it is I who am working to make them useful."

This is the main thrust to our second conversation. I feel the need here to say that I know that there will always be those who will not believe, just as she herself pointed out to me. I can't say that I would blame you. At this point in my limited understanding though, I have no choice but to believe. I doubt that there are many ways to take this belief away from me. I found that by waiting a year and watching events unfold after her death, I have discovered information that has confirmed much of what she had said so early on. I have also found a few discrepancies, but they are small. Normally I am somewhere around 75% to 85 % accurate with most other readings, and I expect this conversation to be comparable. I have questioned her about some of these discrepancies and have received answers that make enough sense that it could also be a case of different perspectives to the same event. If you have no belief that I have spoken to her, close the book now without reading any more. If you are unsure, are fairly sure, or just want to remain open-minded to a later point, enjoy the rest of this odyssey.

CHAPTER 5

The Princess with a Purpose

September 3, 1997: I spoke to the world of spirit again. My guides came forth with a warning that she had a request that what I wanted to know, and what she said to me would remain with me alone unless we chose to work together. They reminded me that it was a gift to me of her trust with her truth and honesty and that she expected the same of me. They told me that I should make this decision for myself and to not allow anyone to make me do what did not feel right within my own being.

> G. "Make all who you feel good about your advisors, but do not let anyone other than yourself make the final choice. It is your will, and your will alone, that must be given and this is of what we are referring."

I again approached Diana with some questions. She agreed to answer them and have them work towards helping me understand why she had need of my services. She also placed a request from herself to me to keep this silent unless we agreed to form *"a union for the betterment of that world. I am going to be brutally honest and would not wish for these answers to become public knowledge unless they are used to make the powerful purpose that I intend to work for a given gift to the world.*" I offered her my agreement. The way I looked at it, if I didn't want to follow through on her request to work with her, why would I want to subject myself to critical scrutiny from the world? Even now I am not sure that I want some of the reactions that this book will create, but have made my choice to press ahead and work with her. In fact, it was her request that I write this book, and she asked numerous times before I found the courage to do so.

R. "Why have you chosen me to be your channel instead of one that must exist within your own country?"

**** "There are many who can receive me if I so choose, but where they live is of no impact. It is who they are and why they are making their gifts work for them. I have considered using someone from the kingdom, but that is not an idea that appeals to me. I feel that if they are of the kingdom then they might have a preconceived idea of what the kingdom should be. This will not make my efforts at changing the kingdom any easier and therefore I am quite happy with one who has no bias towards anything that will affect the kingdom. I am yours and you are mine if that is how we should feel towards one another. It is not where you live, but where you feel the will should be."

R. "What did you mean when you said that you wanted to give the world more of the same as they had given you?"

**** "I was referring to the world's love and the world's faith that I was who they thought me to be. I was not allowed to give them what I wanted due to the restrictions placed upon me by the royal family and the forms of protocol that had been established before I made the world's debut. I still feel the need to return that which was given to me…I wanted to give them love and respect and make them see me for who I was and not who I had to be while the princess."

My next question was whether she would be willing to offer hard, concrete proof that she was who she said she was. Her response was that she could, if needed when the time arose, by giving details of royal family life, her marriage, and her attempts to leave the kingdom that were never given to the media. She says there is enough proof for the royal ones if they need it, but perhaps not the world in general. She said that what matters to her most is that she be able to make those who worked with her on her projects understand that it is she speaking. At this point though, she did not offer me details, but said we would discuss this when we needed to.

R. "You seemed to not want to make your presence known in the first communication. What changed? How and why did you decide to change your mind?"

**** "I was not wanting to make contact with the world for the purpose of making my presence known until I had been given the gift to do so. I am able to say that when I was first over here within this realm, I knew that if I chose to remain silent then I could easily do so….I was given some advice by those who are here and those who were my loved ones on this level. They made me see that I could still be a driving force within my children's world and that I needed to do so if there was to be any future for the kingdom. I am greatly enamored of the idea that I can still make the world better, and possibly even more so, than I would ever have dared dream when upon that world."

I wondered, sometime later that evening, why it was in her mind that she could affect the "kingdom" and the world so powerfully after her death. I wondered if because she seemed to care so much, if she had not considered that the world would not be ready to hear from a dead princess. I knew I hadn't been, and I already had a belief system in place that would allow for such bizarre concepts as speaking to the dearly departed. For those who, because of religious or scientific reasons, had not yet considered such a thing possible, I knew this would sound like the ravings of a mentally unstable individual. I wasn't sure I wanted to submit a résumé for the job of public relations assistant and private secretary to a deceased princess. It was not a job that I had any training for, or that I had ever in my wildest dreams thought would be offered to me.

Again, I had a curiosity. I wondered how she thought this would be possible to give her words out to the world. One day I will learn what most felines don't know: curiosity doesn't just assassinate cute, cuddly kitties; it can do a number on any inquisitive form of animal life. Inquiring minds want to know some things that, in hindsight, might be better left alone. Curiosity has led me to the point of being here at the computer trying to convey to the world what may get me slain—not in the physical body perhaps, but potentially in reputation and credibility.

When I asked her how this could be done, considering I was not a prominent person or a shoo-in for a reception with any of the royals, I had no preconceived ideas. I wasn't that far yet in my thought processes. I was still in shock mode, more or less. Her answer was as follows:

> **** "I have not yet made that a priority for thought…I do not wish for the trade magazines, or those wretched tabloids to get this first, and so I shall ask that you choose not to go that route. I will think this through and give you a better answer after I have made my decision on how we should approach this matter. It will have to be done with some major consideration to the for-

mat and timing. I will seek the answers with my spiritual advisors and give you the answers that you seek another time."

Oh great! The captain of the plane doesn't know where we are going, and I am getting the feeling that the captain isn't sure how and where we are going to land. I started to turn in my boarding pass for a refund, but again, curiosity rears its persistent head. I am surprised that when I look in the mirror I don't see a fuzzy tale and the vertically oblique pupils of a feline in my eyes.

She ends this transcript by asking me to also think on this matter. She makes the statement that we need to arrive at a format that will serve our purpose without causing undue sensationalism. Now, at this point all my fear is wrapped around the thought that to report that you have the words of Diana the Deceased can do nothing but cause sensationalism (negative I am sure!), so I think this is an ironic and humorous statement. I reply that I can agree with that! Her parting remarks include gratitude for my time, and a hope that I can find happiness with my association with her and this work. *So make this time count towards finding that place of being and we will make a good team for the forming of a powerful work.* I must say I greatly admired her consideration for my comfort zone, her confidence in what she had set as a goal, and her positive attitude. I wanted so much to feel one half of what she was projecting to me of the certainty she felt that this project was a good idea. I was personally having a hard time getting to that state of mind.

CHAPTER 6

Forms of Tyranny and Love

W e will start this chapter from transcripts starting on September 5, 1997. I add the date here for it will be important to note these because of some of the information that will come later. I want the dates noted because part of validating this (especially to myself) as having come from a knowing source involves receiving some information before it had reached the public. Perhaps some of the investigators in the case had some knowledge of what may be revealed, but it did not reach me here in America for at least many weeks after having received it. When I began to hear the news reports pertaining to what I already had stored in my computer, I had the feeling of chills, nausea, and tingling. Very similar to what I had experienced at the home of my young friend's mother's house when information I had heard from him had been causally dropped in front of me during conversation. The source was confirming itself to me by having given me prior knowledge of events not yet known. As time progressed more of my stored information came to light, and this is one of the major launching points for the strength of my beliefs and faith to enable me to overcome fear and doubt to write these words to you.

I was mentally blank as to what line of questioning to pursue next, so I climbed back up to the "mountaintop" to ask the wisdom of my gurus. I speak metaphorically, of course, because I usually sit in a very comfortable chair in my office.

I would be too lazy to climb that far for a chat. My guides again gave me several thoughts that had not dawned upon me.

> G. "Our world does not work with the same will to know all that must be given to you for your satisfaction, but we realize that there is a great deal more fear within your world and your own mind about what this world is like....ask her about her intent with the will to make the royal family understand that she is still able to communicate with your world. You are of the feeling she may be wanting to serve her own vendettas with this and we are of wanting you to know if this is of her intent....it is not of a given value to make others feel fear or regret if that is the work that is foremost within someone's mind."

It had been my understanding from several books and metaphysical teachings that in the world of spirit there was an inability to hide one's thoughts from another. I had no way of knowing if my information was correct or the wanderings of another's mind. When in doubt, ask, and so I did. I stated that I had heard that thoughts were pretty well transparent there and that secrets could not be kept. I ask if I had wrong information. They answered, *"It is not that there is an ability to read all that one is capable of thinking, it is that it is possible to make the gift of knowing whether their main intent is for the good or highest ideal available to that entity's vibrational form."*

How is that for an answer that will make you think? I often have to decode their phraseology to access their meaning. Other times their answers are cryptic and the more that you ponder on the answer you stumble upon depth and hidden meanings. I have to love those guys! They keep me thinking and entertained! They assured me that she was of *"good vibrational intent,"* but they wanted me to ascertain if she was of the highest intent.

"We are offering this suggestion to you for the purpose of making you aware of your feelings upon the subject of giving the gift of vindication to her of making the royal family work at giving their will over to knowing that she is of being an even greater power within her death than when she was within their world. That may give you the gift of knowing that when she was working at her own feelings of making them begin to realize that she was a greater force than they had been aware of, she was accomplishing much good through the use of a wrong motivation. There are many things within your world that are of a paradoxical theme such as this and we are trying to make you aware that what one does is of great value, but of greater value if done for the greater good of all involved."

My guides go on to remind me that they allow me the choice to determine whether to work with them for the gift of bringing messages to our world from the world of spirit and to decide how much or how often. They point out to me that *"if there arises a conflict between you and your feelings of making a world contribution, then we will give you the freedom to accept only that which you choose to do.... Think again about our work and realize that all of our work will make you feel some form of conflict, for your world does not readily recognize a form of communicating with this realm and there will always be within your mind that gift of doubt about who and what we really are....begin with knowing that we are of your service and you are of our service and that is of the given rule that those who will serve shall lead and those who lead shall serve."* Many times their words give me the gift of humble spiritual reflection as well.

Taking my guide's lead, as I often do (and sometimes do not, much to their consternation I am sure) I then asked Diana why she wanted the world and her family to know that she was able to communicate. Pretty awesome answer, I think.

**** "I am not going to make that an answer that you might be able to understand, but this is what I have to offer....It was no secret that I gave myself the will to give up on that life many times, but I was always unsuccessful. I was not allowed to come back (to the world of spirit?) until I was able to make an even bigger contribution to the world and this is still what I am hoping to do. I was wanting to make the world see that there were many things that I felt were working against the form of government that we have had since the days when there were not any good forms of government for the protection of the people from those who had the greatest wealth and power. It was for these people that there became a monarchy and this was a good thing only in the minds of those who did not understand that when one is a king there would be, within the context of history, the good and the bad. It was from this concept that there began many future struggles for the kingship from those who would not want another to make the rules, or themselves their subjects. I was given to understand that there were many who were born into the kingship that made their subjects fare no better than before the monarchy was established. I am of the resolution to make the royal family understand that to be a force that can lead, one must do so at the levels of the subjects of whom they are leading.... if there is not a majority that feels their king is offering them protection from the world's harsh forms of tyranny, then they are doing no good for the format that was the foundation of the forming of the monarchy. What this means to those who were born within the guidelines of democracy, I can only guess at.

"I was never very good at making the forms of tyranny that I felt were threatening the kingdom felt by those who wanted to make the monarchy continue as it always had. I feel that I can make these forms of oppression more aware to the royal family by continuing my work with the hungry, the forlorn, the ones who need someone to feel for them when they must face the more pressing needs of their daily lives wondering if they can and will have a future for their children. I am wanting them to see that to work at being king or queen is not to make the kingdom serve the government, but to make the government serve the people."

Having no idea about the English form of government, I asked her if the royal family had any power to change the government over there. I had heard more than once that the monarchy had no real power; they were just a figurehead institution that made very few, if any, policy changes. I was really wishing I had more knowledge of these things. I also felt the need from my pragmatic point of view to ask, that if they did have this kind of power, why would they be willing to let any of this power go? I couldn't truthfully say that I would. Her answer made me realize how badly I was misunderstanding what she was saying. I had thought that she was talking about abolishing the monarchy.

**** "I can see that I cannot make you understand that what I hope to do is not change the form of government, but to change the form of ruling that the royal family has always been entitled to. I will make this example to you… If a man were to go to the palace and ask for a loaf of bread, he would be given the royal escort from the tables of the monarchy without there being anything given to him. I am making this comparison (struck me as similar to the parable of Lazarus and the rich man) to show you that there is not a glitch within our system of government, there is a glitch within the world's view that the monarchy is of greater value than the man who is hungry. I am able to say that I am not going after the royal family for their positions, but for their position on being the ones who are the supreme ones within the kingdom and for their lack of understanding that there are indeed many things that they could do for their country and their own lives if they were but to reach the level of their subjects...greater gifts in giving than being given to. That may sound harsh, but I have been within the royal suites and I know that the concept of giving to others for the work of making their kingdom a happier place for all is not in their understanding for the better part of their thinking....I made my choice that to leave the family was going to be one of the ways that I could give of myself more fully to the people and make a bigger difference for them than being their fairy-tale princess....I am indeed serious with my intent to make my presence known to the royal family for the former thinking to be given a chance to make an exit and the new thinking to make the difference that I know it could."

Told you it was an awesome answer, didn't I?

Ascension Together Water Color © MaMahon 2002

We spoke about Mother Theresa's death next and Diana said, in part, "I was able to make her feel the need that I had to make her my example of being the one who gave me the courage to see that I could do more and that there was no greater favor than getting to make the few who needed us more important than those who would make us think that we couldn't do what we knew in our hearts had to be done." She also said that she was glad that the world was mourning Sister Theresa's loss also and not just the loss of Diana's physical body. About her burial, she had this to say: "I think that if I had made one request about my death it would have been that I be given a simple funeral and more elaborate view of how my life had been for the greater good of many....There is no reason why there has to be such a fuss and a furor over my passing and I want the proceeds of any donations to go to the worthwhile work of making people's lives better while they are living than to making sure that everyone gets to see me being given a formal funeral."

Even with her death, she seemed to prefer a low-key approach. In researching items about her life after I finished most of these conversations with her, I had discovered that she had a hard time accepting the attention laid upon her. Much of the ado about her life was overwhelming for her and the crush of people waiting to see her had unnerved her greatly when she began her reign as the Princess. It was no secret that she sought relief from the incessant media attention to her every move. In time, she had grown into the role and grudgingly accepted the public's adulation. She eventually even grew, or so it would seem, to adopt the old adage, "If you can't beat them, join them." She used the media to cover her worthwhile works as adroitly as they had covered all of the rest of her life. Her not caring that everyone get to see her at death and burial, yet wanting to highlight her causes, seemed very much in character for her.

Our next journey into her words comes from transcripts received on September 7 and 8 of 1997. At the onset of the first set, my guides agree with her assessment of the gifts to be gleaned through her work. "There needs to be a feeling of being guided by the belief that no man is of superiority within the given realm of the making of the sons of God." They relay to me that they wanted me to know that she was of honorable intent with her reasoning for me to decide to accept or decline her offer to me. They also state that if I should decline, it is of no import. I will only be given another assignment. "We will give you another wisdom that is of great benefit for you at this juncture. It is our given intent that if you do not seek to work with this form of making your gifts available to the world, then we will give you but another assignment for your choosing. There is no given pressure for you to make any choice that does not appeal to your feelings as being the way to make the world feel your gifts....There are many ways in which to serve and you have the gift of making the choice that will be right within your own world of service." They made it pretty clear that I could bail on this if I chose, but my mentality has always been to keep the door that Monty Hall offered you instead of gambling with another one. (The baby boomers have to remember "Let's Make a Deal"!) It is always a fifty-fifty percent gamble you are going to get something you'd like, so take what is handed to you and go with it. However, I did allow a year, and some research, to flow by before I made the choice. Fortunately, they didn't set a time limit on me!

Having seen her funeral the day before, I asked her what her opinion had been. Seemed a logical question to ask. In part, her answer is as follows: "I was feeling that there was a great madness with this that I wish I could have avoided, but then again I was never able to make a difference with the mania that seemed to grip people when I was there, so how could I have avoided the will of the masses to make me their fairy-tale princess at my own death?" Her next comments that I will share with you touched me again in a motherly sort of way. "I was allowed to make my presence known to the one who was feeling so sorely grieved that I was no longer there with him and this will be his form of proof that I was not gone, but only a form that had no physical space within his area. It was a gift that I gave to him and was given to me for the purpose of making the duty that he had to perform an event that he could endure. I was honored with the gifts of tribute that were given, but the gift of the feelings of love from all of those wonderful people is something that made me feel even more humility for my many thoughts that I was unloved and quite ordinary." I, as well as you, can only guess to whom she was referring. I assumed by my emotional reaction that it was one of her sons, and my heart tells me that it was Harry, the youngest. Whether he did perceive her, only he may ever know. Much has been said about how well both young men handled the grim duty that they had to perform. I also want to add my admiration to this list. They were exceptional young men showing grace and bravery in unimaginable circumstances. If indeed, as Diana intimated to me, she was able to help them from her realm, what mother would attempt less? If it was so, and only the boys may know this, then I am proud of the mother as well as her sons.

Diana takes a moment to explain how love feels to her in the etheric realm. It was a noteworthy remark, especially for those of us who are exploring the metaphysical world. I am not sure that the full depth of what she says is easily understood by us still of this world. However, I would concede that I do feel that love is felt beyond the body, even when we have one. "This was certainly a new experience to be able to actually feel the love that had been offered to me and to feel the generosity of it. Give me a moment and allow me to explain the way it feels when you cannot feel with a physical body and yet know what you are feeling. There is a powerful form of energy that accompanies love that is not made within the physical body. It is a feeling that there is fullness within your mind and that is a feeling that works without the body and yet is more wonderful than you can imagine. I was well aware of the feelings of being able to love when I was in my body and yet I feel that if I had to feel that again instead of the way I have been made to feel within this realm then I shall say that I have no need to make haste to reaffirm another life within the realm of the living...There are many forms of love within the world and yet there is really only a very weak form of any of them. It is as if there were a fine barrier between the real love of the spiritual world and the world of being in a body that makes the forms of love experienced there seem as if they were the foam instead of the ale. That is a good description, don't you think? I am well pleased with that one."

Yes, I liked it also. What struck me later, after having reread her words about the state of feeling love here versus there, was the eeriness of the scripture read at her funeral by Prime Minister Tony Blair, 1 Corinthians 13:12. Perhaps now we really do only see love through a glass darkly, but then we shall see it for its true depth and beauty.

CHAPTER 7

Destiny, Details, Dying

I offer this next chapter almost verbatim for there is much information that must come from her words and her perspective. This is her account of what she perceived and what she remembers. Again, the dates of this chapter spans material received on September 7, 1997. My emphasis on the notation of dates will become self-evident when the bulk of this material is given to you. Much of what was relayed to me on those dates did not become public knowledge until sometime later. Some of the material given in other areas took months to show up in the media as general public accessibility. I offer this knowing that some of what I have does not match exactly what I have heard reported. However, it was given to me and it is my duty to report it as was given. There is also a chance that what I have may offer further clues, insights, or meaningful information for those who are researching her death. If there are discrepancies in what is written here, I will assume the blame for not having received certain details 100 percent accurately. Let us not forget either that this is her opinion of what happened as she tried to relay it to me. Her view of something may or may not have been the actual case, as in many contrasting eyewitness reports. With this said, let me also say that many things I had been given did, over a period of time, come to light or worked out as she had said it would. This is one of the main reasons I have sat down to hold up this material that she has given to me to the world for their scrutiny.

I asked her to give me a detailed description of the night of the accident. I had been hearing different reports and realized that I could get it from the horse's mouth, so to speak. I will pick up her conversation with her remarks about her "destiny" of dying.

**** "I am able to say that I was not aware that I was going to be leaving the world when I did, or as I have stated, I would have requested that things be kept to a simple level for my funeral. There were many things that I wanted to say and do if I had the chance to know that I was getting to leave, but that is part of the beauty of not knowing. There would be a focus on the leaving and not on the living. I guess that I have come to the wisdom that even though I was able to leave a few things for those who I cared about before I made my way out of the world, I really needed not to know that I was going to die within a given time frame. Then I would have dreaded every moment that I was away from the boys and feelings of being unable to do enough would have consumed me.

"I was able to feel that my life was changing, but that was because I felt that I had found a few new friends and I was going to make the future that I had left be brighter than the one that I had been through. I was going to make myself the wife of someone who I felt really cared for who I was and who wanted me to be his priority. I was going to make the difference that I could without my own life being scrutinized for who I had been and that was what made me think that my life was changing. I am now aware that when I called my mother and told her I was going to make a new life that would be something that I had always wanted, I was making a statement to her and my family that would prove to be fundamentally a major change that no one, even myself, could have foreseen. That was a blessing, I suppose, and that will yet be seen when I give you the details of how I came to make this change."

Here is her claim that she was indeed going to marry. Here is her statement about wanting to dispense with scrutiny of her private life. Here are her thoughts on feeling that life was going to take a major detour for her, but not knowing why she was so sure of that. Here are her words of gratitude for not knowing the time or circumstances of her leaving. I believe that she knew not what actual destiny awaited her but could feel its eminent arrival. Her realization that it was a version of preformed choice will be disclosed later. Let us now continue with her words.

**** "I was given a gift that meant the world to me and that was a gift of the ring that was presented to me with a love that I will always cherish. It was a gift of the man who I had come to love as I had loved no other and I think that perhaps I was given this as a going-away present to make me feel less alone when I made my major life change. It seems that when I was the happiest was when I was given the chance to leave a world that had made me very sorrowful in many of my years. I was at the height of being happy as far as I can remember, and I think that it was a small mercy of God to make me so happy for the time that I had to leave. I was able also to make another so happy and this is also a great source of the gratitude that I feel for the entire series of events that ended my physical life. I was going to tell you that when I was given the ring it was decided that we would not make this public and that was why I was not wearing the ring when we left the hotel. I had placed the ring back into the box and had it given to the man who was to be my protector and husband. There was a security work going on to keep us out of the public eye for that evening, but it was breached by someone whom we must have trusted and that made the whole affair even more pathetic. I was not allowed to wear my new ring and I was not happy with that for I had wanted to wear it to the main wall of the airport for the sake of feeling it against my hand. I was feeling that to make this sacrifice of having to hide our engagement from the world was a further intrusion upon our lives, but this was what was best until we had time to make the announcement to our family and our friends. When it became obvious that we couldn't leave without the press making us, it was decided that would not be prudent, and so we left it."

She mentioned making an attempt to have the press think she was in the area for a benefit the next day, which did little to make them leave her alone the night they were to dine together. She mentions eating chicken eggs (why the distinction?) and something wild, which I understand from reports must have been asparagus (wild?). She says she had thought of ordering a main course of filet mignon but decided she did not want that feeling of being too full. Reports say that she had sole. She mentions an elaborate dessert, something that she says may have been a form of torte, but that she was not ordering. She had no wine with her meal and a very flavorful coffee with dessert. I have no idea if any of this is true. Her description of the flowers on the table is quite detailed.

**** "There were red roses on the table and a yellow type of flower that looked like a few petals surrounded by a green fern with a few yellow flecks on it. It was a lovely arrangement, but I was not familiar with the name of that flower. The flowers were in a glass vase that had a yellow ribbon around it and that made me think of the flowers that we had on our table when we were in Venice for financing a new hospital."

Once again, I have no idea if this has any validity. I haven't seen any information about the flowers or the financing that she has mentioned. I offer this blindly, knowing that it could well stumble those hanging on to a small hold of belief. It had such detail though that I am hoping that someone somewhere can verify some of it. If not, remember that the message is only as good as the messenger understands it. I would accept that my reception was not adequate, for I have made no claims to 100 percent accuracy but feel that the main ideas are intact.

As a matter of fact, later in our chapter, Diana herself will rescind, or at least add to, her original statements to me that I am detailing for you here. It will be given to you as I received them. Let us get on with this next segment of information. Again, the details were many and will perhaps serve to justify me or hang me. Either way, I have faith that I am doing the right thing here.

Be prepared. Some of her next utterances to me I found very chilling. They still are as I cover them for you. I was emotionally drained at the end of this session.

> **** "I was able to see that if we left then the reporters and the paparazzi would see us, so I suggested that we wait on the other side of the hotel for another friend of Dodi's to arrive with another car and make our escape through the main area of deliveries. It was a good plan, except that the hotel forgot to get another driver lined up for this so we called a friend of Dodi's to come and make our escape. There was quite a ———

(Did not get this word clearly. Perhaps "crush"?) of confusion about who would ride with us and I insisted that I make the choice of my own bodyguard. I feel sorry now that I made him be with us; but then again I was aware of the defenseless feeling I had in these situations. We are in the car leaving as a group of paparazzi come from nowhere and make us the objects of their attention. It was like a thousand times before and we were trying to make them give up the chase. I was feeling that we could hurt someone if they made the wrong move so I insisted that we get well away from them for the safety of those involved.

"I was not aware we were coming upon the tunnel until it was beginning to loom over us, then I heard the driver shout something and the world seemed to make a bizarre race forward. There was a grinding sound, a feeling that we were taking off in the Concorde. Then came a total rush of pain and of making the trip without an airplane. The front seat came up into my face; the feeling was that I was going to go through the windshield. There was a sickening sound of the air being forced out of all our lungs and the movement of everything going upside down. I was not aware of the next few minutes, I think, because I felt the feeling of making myself come up out of a foggy sleep and the pain making me go back down. I was able to feel myself being given instructions to stay still and I was able to become aware of the many people who were talking around me, but I have no real memory of this time. I made an effort to come about when I heard someone call my name and there was a man who kept telling me I was going to be all right. I was not able to think clearly, but I knew

I was not going to be. I felt that I was losing control of my senses once again and I believe I tried
to tell someone to make me a gift of making my
last words to my family."

Has this passage affected you as it has affected me? It was hard
to receive this and still focus on typing. Even though I had asked for
a detailed account of that evening, I had not considered the emotional ramifications of having her tell me about the accident. I guess
I thought that there would not be an actual account of the physical
sensations and sounds of the accident itself. Whatever my thoughts
had been going in to this, I was not prepared. This was a glimpse to
me of how it must be to be a journalist. You cover an event, or ask a
question, trying to be objective, but find yourself fighting your own
subjective emotional reactions. Those who cover war, child abuse,
murder, etc., must be strong and well trained to remain analytical
and concise. I would be a sobbing mess in no time.

This was delivered to me within a week, give or take a day, from
her death. I believe that not all of the details of how the accident had
occurred had been released at this point. In this passage, we have not
only her account that she insisted that they try to outrun the photographers, but the statement that she had mentioned the waiting
on the other side of the hotel. Her comment about "the grinding
sound" has me wondering if this was when they struck the other car
since she then follows with the description of "taking off," as in going
airborne. Then comes the pain, a result of rapid deceleration, and
being thrown about the car. The "flight without an airplane" is an
apt enough description of what happens to any occupant of a vehicle
that stops immediately upon impact with an immovable object while
not restrained by a seat belt. The order of her description does indeed
fit with what I later learned to be details of what the investigators
discerned to be the circumstances of the accident.

I have heard many conflicting accounts on the subject of these
"last words." Some sources claim there was a message, others say that
it was impossible. Perhaps her account is only what she thinks happened in her on-again, off-again battle with consciousness. Her mind

may have wanted to express words to them, but the physical body was not able to respond. I had a similar experience while under anesthesia for dental surgery. I could hear the team working on me, feel them working on me, and was screaming to them to stop, but not a word escaped my mouth. I was unable to even open my eyes or move anything to let them know I was awake, but I was able to repeat their operating room dialogues with amazing clarity. They were surprised, to say the least!

Now, back to Diana's account of the rest of this evening/early morning. Again, much of this may stretch your currently held belief systems but continue with your open-minded approach that you have adopted when choosing to read the rest of this book.

The best way to judge is to hear the whole case and then weigh the evidence carefully.

> **** "I was given a feeling that there were many around me and I think I felt them opening my chest and making my blood warm. I was able to feel them working on me, but the pain was as if it were somewhere else. I was given a few moments that I remember clearly and I wanted to tell them to tell my sons that I was always with them and that I would always make them my guiding reasons. I was not able to tell this person that I was going to make them feel me and that I would be there when they came to see me."

I question, as well as you do, that she really had a conversation while undergoing open heart massage. Either the order of her story is confused, or her "words" were not for those of this realm. She goes on to say that she felt great relief that she saw someone that she recognized because she was afraid that she would die alone and no one would be there who knew her. It has crossed my mind about the accounts of those on their deathbeds who speak to those of their deceased loved ones, or some other person, that are not visible to the rest of us. I experienced this when my own father died. He spoke to his sister and another who made him smile shortly before he died. Perhaps her remembered conversation was not with anyone in the hospital room where her rescuers valiantly fought to bring her back. I leave this thought with you as another possibility to explore while mulling over her words given above. She continues:

> **** "I was given a gift of feeling no pain as I left my body and then I could see that I was not able to make the surgeon aware that I was behind them. It is a very clear memory that I have of seeing myself there and yet knowing that I was not going to live. I felt like making them stop, but they continued to make me try to live for another many minutes. I was aware also of the group trying to give me their strength, and their fears that they weren't being able to make any difference. I felt the wave of pain from them as they decided to make the attempts come to a halt and that was a painful thing for me to experience. I was not feeling sad or much of anything for my own self, but I seemed to be feeling their grief."

This next segment of the transcript will contain some information held by one of those who were in the room with her. Perhaps the one she speaks of will know of what she refers, but again this may only be Diana's perception of the event. If, however, it does spark recognition in this person, please contact me. I would love to hear your side of it!

> **** "I was able to make the one who came to my left side feel me, I think, because she turned around and looked at my form, then left the room. I was aware of her feelings of fear and then her feelings felt as if they moved over into the realm of being worried. I think she felt me but would not let herself make the connection

out of fear. I saw her eyes widen and felt her fear. I felt greatly sorry that I caused her to feel this. I was around her form and then she looked at me with her eyes wide and I knew she felt what I was feeling. She felt to me as if she were made of fiber that was thin, but enough to make you feel it, but not thick enough to stop you from falling through. There was also a fragment of time that I was feeling myself being pulled into another area and then I was given a gift of making the world of spirit an awareness around me. I was then given the instruction to wait for a while to make the gift of trying to connect with someone, but that was only a few moments, or so it seemed."

It is here that I had to take a break from our session. I was unable to return to our conversation until the next day, September 8, 1997. It would seem that in the time that had expired, she was able to clarify some of her memories, or that she found she remembered other details. She also offered an interesting account of how memories are accessed in that realm without having a physical brain to store them in. Our next chapter will take us into her depth of memories and her reasoning for her death.

CHAPTER 8

Memories, Remorse, Conspiracy

The next day I returned to our conversation by asking my guides to assist with the connection. They instruct me to again make her aware of my need to know that it is she who is communicating with me and to let her know that they are my guiding group. I asked them why they wanted me to tell her these things and why they did not do so themselves.

> G. "We are wanting you to do this for the purpose of making her aware that we are of her service if she will but ask for our assistance. There is a given rule that when one reaches this level there may only be contact with those who are of the same guidance group unless there is a giving of the will for the others to make the connection. It is our purpose to connect you with her, but it is only because we are of your guidance group. There are those of her guidance group who are working with her and they are the ones connecting us to her. Allow her to know that we too can make the connection with her if she is making the request for this to occur. This is the way that we must make the declaration to her of our intent…

so that she may more fully know the extent that
we play within her connection to you."

When I have the connection with her, and after some other
conversation, I tell her the message from my guides. She says that she
is aware of them when we speak and could tell they were not the ones
who spoke to her. She says that she has no need of them until she is
more use to working with the ones who are working with her then.
She finishes this discussion by saying: "It is too confusing to make
conversation with too many and I get lost sometimes in the feelings
and voices that I am already dealing with. Thank them for their offer,
and I will consider them at a later point if I have need."

We next launched into the meat of our conversation. I had asked
her if she was ready to resume our conversation, and indeed she was.

**** "I am ready and am able to make you
of being more explicit with my answer to you
on the events of my death. I was able to make a
connection with the earlier memories that I have
of the evening that we were killed. I was able to
think about the scene and then I was given a
flood of images about the evening, so let us make
another attempt at being clearer with my previous answer.

"I was able to make the connection to why
I was so well oriented during the accident and
why I remember the feelings so well....I was able
to make the connection to the accident with my
emotions and not the rest of the evening except
for the emotional parts of the memories. I was
capable of giving myself the will to go back
through the evening with the emotional aspect
of the evening, but not the moments that gave
me no emotional feelings that would not make
an impression. I was given the advice to make
myself remember the aspects that were unevent-

ful emotionally and I must now rescind the version that I had given you before. I was well aware that I was going to be given the ring, but I do not think that I expected it that evening. There had been a gift that I had given him and he had made the comment that he had a small gift for me when we dined together that evening. I had not expected it to be the ring that we had spoken of, but that was his way. He loved to surprise people for the feelings that he could make them happiest if he gave them something they were not expecting....I was aware that he had a gift for me, but I was not prepared for the ring and for the gift of his proposal upon that particular night. I was so given over to emotion that I was able to remember that aspect of the evening very clearly and I think that I was reporting to you upon that with much clarity.

"What I do not feel that I remembered clearly enough was the way that we were to leave the hotel and why we were leaving in the manner that we did. I was giving you the things that I seemed to remember, but now I have that I was confused as to why we had been leaving without the others who had been with us. It was reported that there were reporters and photographers waiting for us and to make our escape we had to make a switch in our original plans. I was given the choice of who I wanted to escort us from the hotel and I made the decision for the one who had been so kind to me and for his appearance. He seemed to remind me of my brother, and I felt a special feeling that he would make the evening more special when we were being transported...He was a fair man and had many times been given an assignment that he was not fond of, but he had the grace and dignity to make his opinion known to no one. I was able to read his feelings because I am fortunately able to read people with a gift that is not often made available to many that I know.

"I feel great remorse at having him with us now, for he is the one who will suffer the most since we are now beyond the feelings of pain. If you choose to work with me, I would wish to make a statement to him for my gratitude that he was with us and how sorry I feel that I caused him to be with us. I was also going to say to you that when I said he was a bodyguard for me, I was not making the claim that he was my personal bodyguard, he was my personal choice."

I next asked her how the photographers knew that they were leaving the hotel, and where they were when her party exited the door. I was trying to get as much detail as I could about this whole evening and the events surrounding that fateful car ride.

**** "I was going to make that another part of my answer to you, so let us continue....It was a given that we would leave with the other car, but when the time came it became obvious that if we left then it would be a media madhouse, so we chose to wait for the other car and driver to arrive. I was the one who suggested that we leave from another area of the hotel and that made us less vulnerable to the media onslaught that was waiting outside the hotel. There was a call placed to the driver and he was notified to make the former works of security void and make the new arrangements for pick up.

"It was a well-conceived plan, but then again there is a relentlessness to the media that one does sometimes underestimate. I think the other car left and several of the reporters and media sharks followed, but there must have been some who made the connection that we weren't there with the other entourage. I do not really know where the paparazzi were that began to follow us, because I felt we had been able to make the car without being seen except by few. Then suddenly the flashbulbs and faces trying to peer into the car surrounded us. I was the one to give the order to make them go away and I feel that our driver thought I meant at all cost. I was not afraid of them getting pictures as much as I was concerned that one of the fellows would be crushed if they made a wrong move. I think that if I had it to do all over again I would have stopped the car and had them make all of the pictures that they wanted."

It is interesting that she states that she was the one to give the order to get well clear of the photographers, and that the driver was only following her order. I find it noteworthy that I could detect no ill feelings for the man who had been the driver and had, as such, driven them to their deaths. I was never aware of any emotional tone of blame or anger connected with the driver. The essence of the emotion behind what I received was that she was willing to accept the blame for this course of action, and therefore wished she had let the media get what they were after. Even though there might be some form of recrimination, of sorts, towards the media for hounding her, note again that she had their welfare foremost in mind. This has confirmed for me that her image as a caring and gentle person has much validity. During all my conversations with her, I had always sensed a gentleness about her that would be hard to define or compare. Let us continue with her words.

**** "It was not for me that I cared, but for the boys and the publicity that they would be subjected to. I was trying to protect them while living the life that I wanted, and now I feel that I have made them even more sorrowful by foolishly thinking that I could have a private life that would not include the media. I am feeling like I should explain here that I was not keeping my relationship with Dodi from my sons. I think the boys were fond of Dodi and would have been happy if they got to make him their stepfather. I would never have made the decision to marry him if there had been any doubt about my sons' ability to accept him and make them happy. I was not running from the media to keep the affair quiet from my sons, but to keep the world from making their lives miserable from all of the exposure. I was wrong to assume that we could escape that, and it has cost me much for my sons. As I have said, I am not unhappy that I no longer live in my body, I am just very distraught at having caused my sons so much needless pain. Thank you for this well given bit of venting my frustrations and I will continue my answer to you."

Again, her concern for her sons is well evident. It was touching to me that she felt the need to thank me for listening to her "frustrations" because I was hanging on every word from her. I was the one who felt that I should be thanking her for the privilege of her speaking to me and being so open and personal. I felt a sense of great honor. I was growing in respect and admiration of her with each conversation, not because she had been a princess, but for the person that I was experiencing through her words and emotional resonance.

Gratitude is inferred in her next words for those who came to the aid of those in the car. These words are eerie for me to read even now, although I can only imagine the scene and emotions of all involved at this point. Being in conversation with her naturally throws me into the role of sensing what she is saying and how it must have been for her.

**** "I was made aware of the tunnel only when I saw the floor and the seat go dark as we approached the entrance. I think that I made an attempt to face forward when I heard the driver scream something and then the world went forever changed. I remember also the sound of a few quick words from the bodyguard and I think then we must have hit the pillar. I will not regress into the former description of the accident for I have given an accurate enough account of the events that I remember but will move forward to the well-intended efforts of making me live. There were many people who came forward to try and help us and I think that I have a partial memory of one of them making me comfortable by being there. I was not always aware of the moments in chronological order, I am sure, but there happened to be a fellow who seemed to make me his priority as far as giving me a hand to hold and a hand with his kind words to me. I was holding on to consciousness very poorly and I feel I made the mistake of focusing on the wrong things.

"I am not aware that I was in a feeling of being able to think clearly and I may have said some things that were not coherent. I was trying to tell someone to make my sons feel me around them and then I remember seeing the face that I knew. I was so overwhelmed with the emotional fear of knowing that I was dying that I didn't make a conscious connection to who he was, but I knew he knew me. I wanted him to make my last words to my sons and to my brother…

As I have said, I wanted the boys to know that I would always be there if they needed me, for I had a surety of mind that I could make God feel that I needed to be there for them. I was also feeling that if they knew that I would always make them my priority then they would have the benefit of believing that even from heaven I would be smiling for them. I was not overly concerned with telling them that I loved them, for it was not words that they needed to hear to know this, but the fact that because I loved them they would always be the focus of my heavenly life as well.

"There was no way that I could change the outcome, whatever that would be, for my life or the losing of it, but they could be the ones who would make the outcome of what happened mean something to their lives. I was able only to make them feel me when they were alone, but they felt that I was there for them to make them see that they needed to be strong....I am sure that they are receiving enough instruction to be strong and do not wish to compound this with the feeling that I want them to be so regimented that they must deny their feelings of deep sadness and grief that we have parted. I feel that when I make my presence known to them again, it will be when they know that I am able to be with them if they are of need....It is my intent to make them aware of this field (realm?) and let them know that I have no regrets except for leaving them, but that shall be another thing that I will need to approach with great care as to how it should be done."

The conversation takes another turn after some more expressions of gratitude to me for giving her my time and comments about my decision-making process with regard to working with her towards a public forum for her words. I will pick up the rest of her statements at the last of these comments.

> **** "Give me your word that you will not make your decision based solely on the facts that you will glean from the world of television. I think you will see that what I have said is going to be made public when there is a further investigation of the events of that evening. What was so plain to me with the accident was that we were not being pursued only by the paparazzi but by another vehicle with the well-defined markings of a foreign vehicle, other than the ones that I was familiar with. It was a gray or silver blue vehicle and had a very large windshield with the insignia of a foreign language on it. I was noticing it making the same form of turns that we were making and it seemed to be keeping pace with us. If they find out whom that car may have had in it, it would make the investigation take another forward thrust towards finding out what happened."

Talk about being surprised by these statements! It would seem that she was giving me an identification of another car that could have been involved. At this point, there was no talk on the news of another car. This caused me great concern because I had not heard anything about another car. The media was reporting about the motorcycles and photographers being held suspect, pending a further investigation. I did not know what to think of these words from her.

However, her words reminded me of the first words ever spoken to me by her. In her third or fourth sentence to me, she had said, "I think I was killed for this reason." I had forgotten to ask about that statement, even though it had caught my attention at the time it was spoken. Now, in light of these newest words, it sparked my memory about the statement of being killed for some reason. So, I hurriedly asked her to clarify that first statement about being killed.

> **** "I am unable to remember why I said that except to say that I was fairly certain at that time that I had been killed to keep me from making the royal family feel any more of the power that I had begun to use...I do not feel that I was a marked woman from the royal family itself, but there were powers that had a vested interest in me not becoming the force that I knew I could be with my works of humanitarianism. I think there could have been a conspiracy to keep me from making any more of the royal family look and feel any more powerless in the face of the royal watchers making the comparisons that had begun to circulate. I was not aware that the royal family had any harsh feelings towards the work that I was doing, but I had been advised that there was a faction amongst some of the political powers that could be very displeased with the image that I was creating. There could be proof of this if there is ever an investigation into the whereabouts of the car, but that will remain to be seen. I have the counsel of my fellow friends here in the spiritual world to make me see that if that were the case, then I was only making the form of my death more dramatic to further accomplish something that I needed to do. It was an interesting thing to make that assumption, but they say that all is planned for a reason and I was consenting to the purpose and the mode of my departure."

Again, I can make no claim to the truth of these words, but I feel very strongly that they should be put forth in print so that others may decipher for themselves what they feel or know about the content of them. I do not think that any of this should be dismissed solely for the fact that some facts do not match exactly with what is known. There are many things that are unknown and some key or clue might be found within this correspondence. I have no way of knowing, so I have set forth to record these words simply for the purpose of giving them out to those who might.

Her words about the other car, although not matching the description of the white Fiat which later came to be mentioned by the media, does not mean that there was not another one of her description. Remember, from her words about watching the motorcycles and not seeing the tunnel looming, that she was apparently facing toward the rear of the car. She may never have seen the white Fiat for her attention was drawn elsewhere to another vehicle. Or perhaps a white car looks gray/silver through tinted windows at night? This account is meant only to stimulate thought for those who are interested, or who have the power to find out if her words to me make any sense.

I have, as I said, seen some verification to some of these many words contained within my transcripts. I feel that to not offer these things would be a wrong thing to do. More wrong possibly than facing the derision that may accompany disclosing them if there would be no validity. As I have said to my intimates who knew of the existence of these transcripts, "I think I would rather live with the 'I did' than the 'I did not' of this whole business." That was another of my deciding factors when making the leap across the chasm of fear in writing this book for release to the public.

CHAPTER 9

The Foundation, Fun, and Fergie

We will start this next section of transcripts with words from my guides. At this point in my abilities, I always went to my guides for a connection; although later, I found I could go directly to her. It was the guides who finally tipped me off that I could connect directly. I do not know if I could have from the beginning or if over time the connection between she and I grew strong enough not to need a link. I include the words from the guides to show that they were helping me monitor what was going to become of the work with Diana. They were, as they are supposed to do, looking out for my interests, even with working with someone of this stature. They want me to be well informed in my decision-making process and to truly evaluate what I wish to do.

G. "She must work at being made aware of the consequences that you feel this assignment will have for your life. We would suggest that she be given your wisdom on why you must make certain that she is of great intent and that she is making the plans for this arrangement to be of benefit for you also. It will not do well for her to be unaware of your concerns and this is our intent for your session today....We want your will to be that which will be of highest wisdom and of highest will guidance to know that you are making a momentous decision....Our world does not wish for this to be the way to make the gift to the world that there is communication available to your world if that would be a hindrance upon your own will for your life."

When the connection is established between Diana and myself, Diana asked to speak before I ask any more questions. We will pick up the most important aspects of her statement to me.

**** "It is a good deal of thinking that I have done on why we should make my contact to you available to the world and therefore I have decided that we should try, if you are of agreement. There are many things that are given to another human being if there is no feeling that they are going to remember them if they die. It is a form of tyranny to allow others to starve to death, to allow others to make their exit out of the world through improper medical care, to make the children feel that they have no hope for a brighter future than what they must see their parents cope with. I feel that our work would make many see that if I can be wanting to change things even now after I have left that world, then they must assume more responsibility for these things while they are yet there. I am therefore suggesting that we give them these things to make them aware that if there is inequality within the world, then there is an awareness of it within this one. It would do well to make them see that if I can be there through my thoughts to you, then there are others here who are making them accept responsibility for their actions. I do not want this to sound morbid, but if I were to rest in peace as they have said over my body, then I must make the changes that I so desperately wanted to when there.

"I was unaware of the world of spirit to a very great extent within my earthly life, and I have come to realize that if I had been more aware I would have done things with a more spiritual mind for the outcome. I am very sorry that I have done things that will make my sons feel the criticism that they will encounter someday, but then I was not a very spiritual person. I was a product of the thinking that if I could make myself happy then I could make them happy.

"I was looking for the way to happiness for many years and I feel I focused upon the physical approach far more than I should have, and when I did find that making a difference to others made me happy, I was beginning to work with the spiritual approach....I am now going to make you a gift of knowing that I am of serious intent to make you the spokesperson for this work and I think that you are of making this decision also, but if I am wrong, then I am regretful to have made the wrong assumption. Are we of the same mind with this, or are we missing the bond that I have come to feel with our speaking to one another?"

R. "You are not mistaken with the bond that we have formed through our conversation for I feel it too. I am not sure that I have made the decision to make this my work....The problems that I have with it is not knowing how we are to do it, how it will affect my life and the lives of my family, and if there is the true good in it that we hope and dream of. I must also consider that if you are who you say that you are and your supposition that you were killed for the works that you did might be true, then those same people will be none too thrilled with this work or me either. Why did you feel that you were killed? What led you to that assumption?"

Notice again how I want some clarity on her statement that she felt she had been killed. This was a major point of consideration for me as to whether to become involved in this proposed project or not. I hope my caution did not derive from watching too many Mafia or spy movies, but the thought had entered my mind that to do this might not be good for my health. I wanted another dose of her thoughts upon this subject. It was also a good way to cross-reference her words to look for errors or lack of continuity. Being analytical by nature, I was always trying to find a way to explain to my intellect, at this point, what I felt with my heart. Her words fit with what had been said previously in a seamless flow, so my intellect was satisfied, but these words of hers did not exactly stabilize the level of my concern.

**** "I am not sure that is what happened, but as I have said, there is a feeling I have that the car which I saw was not of our group, and if it was not, then why was it following us and making sure that it stayed with us? I was also forewarned that there would be attempts towards making me cease the work that I was doing. I was not given the reasons why they wanted to make me quit except that I was causing an unfavorable opinion towards the other royals for not being as diligent with their works for humanity. Perhaps it was the work itself. I was meddling in things some wanted me well away from. I was not going to let it deter me and I am still not, but it is true that there was a feeling that I had that I was made to die for being who I wanted to be.

"I am told here that I was in accord with the events and I feel that I must have been for I am not unhappy with this world....I was a good and feeling person and wanted to make a large difference in the world. I was able to do this very well with my fame, but the world was so vast and the workers so few. I feel that I agreed to come here to make an even bigger impact on the world and that is why I am suggesting this arrangement. We will continue with the questions that you have."

Here was an opportunity to find out the thrust of the future of this proposed work. I was still in the dark as to the ideas she had for her work, and I needed to know this for my decision-making process.

Make note in this next section how it flows easily into some humor and friendly banter. I was impressed with her gift of making me laugh and her apparent attempt to put me at ease with her and this work. She was trying to lighten up my very serious mind-set over talking to someone like herself. It was, as I have inferred before, a very odd feeling. I did not know which way to respond other than as a secretary or amateur reporter. After our little exchange in this conversation, I felt far more at ease and encouraged to be more of who I normally am.

R. "What type of guidelines do you wish to establish for your works that you started? Give me some examples so I will have some idea of what this will be about."

**** "I will make the statements that if they are to use my name in connection with any of the projects that I have started, then they must accept those who come regardless of their stature and their political beliefs. There is to be no will to turn away anyone if there is a need and that if they are to make the gifts work to their fullest they must give them equally to all who apply.... If they were to use these for the purpose of making the world benefit then they must divide these up amongst the world and not unduly so to the United Kingdom. I am well aware that if they wanted they could make the United Kingdom their top priority, but that would not be my wish. It is wrong to make someone suffer based upon the area of their birth, and I wish to make this known to the ones who are delegating the funds to be used in my name.

"I want equality for the world, not an imbalance toward the causes of the United Kingdom, just because I had been their princess. It is wrong to use monies sent from all over the world for the strengthening of the United Kingdom while those of other worlds go without. I will also make it known to those with whom I have worked personally that I will make them aware of my presence if they should need me to help them with their work. This is a pledge that I have made to them for the executing of my wishes. I am content that this is a fair and reasonable thing to ask, and that if we can make them feel my presence within their hearts, then there will be great works done in my name for the world's benefit. It will perhaps have vindicated the errors that I have made within that world and I would be able to rest in the peace that they so fervently wish for me.

"I am happy that you are wanting to know this and I will make you a list of the guidelines when our work has begun. I am your fan for your ability to make this seem so normal when we both know that for others it would be a formula for being committed to an institute for the less than able to deal with the world on a normal basis."

R. "Hey, don't joke about that! I could be placed there if the world thinks this is crazy. I am only kidding, but then again, maybe I'm not!"

**** "You are a funny person and I can use your humor to make the world see that if they think death is so final and sad, then they haven't met with the right ideas. I was feeling like we should form a pact between us that if this is given to the world that we do so with some form of humor and frivolity so that there can also be some laughter for the world over this situation. I was honored by the world's sadness, but I feel that if they could have laughed about the irony of the world's favorite princess making the headlines with her feet over her head than there would have been a good feeling for me that I was able to bring them some form of laughter also. I was always made to be so serious and I think if I could have laughed more then I would have been a happier person.

"I was always finding the irony in things that would make me laugh, and that is part of who I truly am. Our work should make people feel good and I wish you would lighten up with your feelings that this is such a serious conversation. I was able to make you finally laugh, and I think that I have made another feeling of commonality between us. I am your friend also and this is what friends are for, don't you agree?"

R. "Yes, I love my friends for the laughter that we share. I think that we are becoming friends for I am able to see that we share a love of irony. But you have to remember that I am a little overwhelmed at the thought that I am speaking to THE princess, much less that you are now dead. I felt like I had to be serious. It helps me keep the perspective. I wasn't going to approach the princess of Wales with jokes about her life or her death. How was I to know that you couldn't have ordered me beheaded, or some such thing? (My attempt at humor in this instance!) Thanks for allowing me to feel more at ease in this conversation. It will be lots more fun, won't it?"

**** "I am capable of still making the world seem like a funny place to myself and that is a freedom that is giving me much fun right now with the things that I have acquired over here. For instance, did you know that if you think real hard about someone here that they have to make themselves available to you? Think about the times that we have thought about someone and then given them a piece of our minds. Isn't that funny to know that they hear us and they can't shut us up? What about the times that we make a mistake and think no one saw us? It wasn't funny when I first came here because I realized with horror that I had made some pretty awful mental statements of some of my former friends and family members. I then realized that they had likely done much the same thing. It was funny to me after that. I can't wait to hear all the thoughts that get sent my way! This should make me laugh all the more."

No, I had not realized the full implications of what she had just covered. I knew that I could converse with those of the spirit world but had not taken the thought on through to how much of our thoughts they might really hear. Almost made me paranoid about what I had thought of some of the deceased, but I only hoped they were able to see the humor in it as she had done. What a gentle reminder that our thoughts may be heard by those who are not here. I now monitor myself far more carefully!

Our conversation took a more serious turn soon after this. I again slipped into role of questioner and asked her a question that had been spawned by some comments I had heard about Sarah Ferguson returning to attend Diana's funeral. It seemed that the reports of this event had touched upon a dispute, or falling away, between the two of them. I, myself, was curious about the reason, but thought that perhaps this also could be a good basis for verification. I asked her about the fact that I had heard about a falling out between them. She did answer me, although I have no clue if this answer means anything or not.

All of her words will not be given here, but here is the main gist. She says that when they did feel friendship that they were the best of friends. Much of what Diana says has to do with her position of Sarah Ferguson leaving the "kingdom" and her own feelings associated with it. She makes the statement that little did she know that in the future that Sarah's courage would be a beacon for her in her own leaving of the family fold. Diana says that she bears the greater burden for the estrangement, and why. She had great joy that Fergie returned for her funeral because it showed her, and the world, that they could still be able to feel great things for each other if they had given it the chance to reblossom.

I chose to not include this verbatim for I again feel this is almost a private conversation that should be held in trust. It concerns someone that I have no access to. I cover it here only as a closing of this section of transcript, not as a full disclosure to the world at large. The actual words shall only be given to the subject of the conversation.

CHAPTER 10

Mental Movies, Mischief, Merciful Motivations

The date of this transcript is September 11, 1997. It is still less than two weeks after her accident. Much has occurred within our conversation and already I have been asked several times for a decision about working with her to bring her words to the public. I am never one to jump impetuously into any situation. I could not make a decision of this magnitude in such a short time span.

I begin this session of connecting to Diana by asking my guides if they wouldn't just this once tell me what to do. From prior experience with them, I knew that they had never given me the command to do anything, or a direct answer on what to choose. They had always given guidance, but never a flat-out, firm, final answer towards what I should do. I was silently hoping that this would be the one exception. I state that there are too many unknowns for me to decide, and it was too tough for me to make myself. Oh well, so much for hoping that a definitive answer would be given to me in a firm commanding yes, or even a simple explicit no!

G. "It is our will that you be given this wisdom. It is of your will that you became the one who will receive with such clarity all of those within the world of spirit. There is no reason that you cannot make a decision with this on your own. We are of understanding that you are well informed with how you feel with this, and we are of great pride that you are so able to make the emotional connection that you have with that which is our world. It is of your credit that you have come so far as to not only receive the words, but the infliction of the words and the emotional tone of these words.... It is many who can receive the thoughts, but there are not many who can receive the feelings and therefore know the truest meaning behind the reception of the words.

"We are of the understanding that you are working with the realm of rational thought with this, but there is also a feeling to us that you are working the rational thought within the basis of what you feel to be accurate. It is a future that you must embrace, for when working with the world of spirit there is not a clear form of proof that may be given with the identity of those who will approach you and you must work at assessing this information through the channels of what you feel of their energy essences.

"We are of the opinion that you are working well with the information that is being given to you and are of being well pleased with the gifts of attention you are giving this assignment, even if it should not be your will to work with her for her public forum that she is wanting to accomplish."

R. "What do you think of the consequences if I take the assignment to go public? Can you give me any insight as to how this would be received, and what the future of this project may hold?"

G. "It is not our intent to work with you on these questions, for the future is determined by those involved and their wills of which we cannot determine. It is, however, adequate that we say that you have the feelings that it will be well received within the circles that will matter most and this is an indicator of the future events.... No guarantees that all will be well for there will be those who can and will refuse to accept this for they are of not wanting the world to change. It is a form of fear for many, that to change is to make themselves feel less than secure. It is therefore their intent to make the world remain as it is, in fear of not knowing that the changes that she purposes would be of greater benefit for the masses....It will make those who are the ones who work at being the oppressors feel their own burdens of guilt and that is a form of feeling that no one upon your world wishes to feel voluntarily."

Diana then enters into conversation with me and offers some things from her childhood that may well serve as forms of proof. She acknowledges that these were not known by the public and can be verified only by those who were involved and who have heard her speak of these things. Once again, I find myself offering information that I cannot verify and realize the risk that I take by doing so. However, this work is as much about faith and feelings for me as it is about facts and data. I offer these things in faith of my feelings about these communications even when I have no verified facts or substantiated data.

**** "I can give you even more details that will make you feel that I am who I say that I am. There is a gift that I am learning to access over here that will take some time to master, but it is a great feeling to make the world that you have left seem like your own personal, private showing of a great movie. There is a way that if you think of something or someone, then you can review that which is of that essence and watch the words and the feelings go through your mind like a movie screen. There is a scene that I remembered after I had accessed that memory and I will share this with you."

She then tells a tale that may have happened when she was five or six years old. It was not publicly known, and only few may know of it. It involved an attempt by a young child to give comfort to horses, and how the attempt got out of hand due to her not understanding the consequences of her actions. She says that she was not punished for this, but that she shall remember the feelings of forlornness, fear, and guilt associated with this event.

**** "It is a funny thing that when you get here it is not the entire life that can be remembered. This is because the memories of any life are recorded in the brain, but when you die there is only the remembrances of the emotional aspects of the events that made an indelible impression within your psyche. I was able to access this memory by going into the memory banks that are stored within my own soul. As you can well imagine, this was an event of great effect upon me for the forming of a major level of feeling. I have remembered other things that are of great impact upon who I became, and feel that if I got started I could remember enough to make a book the size of the encyclopedias.

"I will tell you of another major thing that I happened upon that shall also be good proof of what I was to become with the meaning of what this lesson taught me. I was around five or six when this occurred also, I believe. I think I was able to remember this because I was able to make the connection through thoughts of my older sister. I was thinking about her when I remembered her giving me one of her dolls to make a few more children that I was going to teach. I was making the children feel their lessons of discipline, and when I spanked her doll it became a shambles in my hands. It fell apart and I remember the horror that I felt when I had to tell her that I had killed her doll.

"I was in tears and I remember thinking that if I ever had any children I would only be kind and loving to them and never cause them any hurt. I feel that this is my earliest impression that if you mistreated a child that they would self-destruct in your hands and that made me who I was with my own children and the children that I encountered.

"I was always seeking to make up for the guilt that I felt over this incident and wanted to mend all of the broken little children within the world. It is another thing that made me who the world thought of as the fairy-tale princess, for I had a compassion for children that could not be denied within me.

"Thinking of these things serves to make me even more dedicated to the purpose of working with the world of form so that another child may be given services and made to feel less alone, scared, hungry, and unloved. There are millions of broken little children who need fixing. The world needs to see that if there is to be a happy ending for this princess there must be a form of fixing them for me to feel the gift of being the one who was able to make the feelings of being abusive go away within the mind of the little girl who made her own charge self-destruct with her cruelty.

"I was moved by this incident to be another person who vowed to never hit another child, and I think I expanded that into being a person who never turned her back upon another child. I am giving you these things for the purposes of making me seem less like the fairy-tale princess who had no flaws, but the person that I really was. I was only a scared little girl who had to grow up far more rapidly than I would have had to if I had chosen the commoner's way of life instead of the life that made me into the princess of the century....I had many things that I had to exorcise from within my psyche that made me who the world came to see. I was never able to correlate the person I was reported to be with the person that I innately was. I was packaged for the public and I made that work for me in the end. I was able to turn that which I loathed into the fuel for the life that I wanted to make, to ease the pains deep within me.

"It is so healing to be able to make this discovery, even now, and I am of deep gratitude for the feelings that I have been able to attain over here. There would be so much less fear of death if the masses could be more aware of the real peace and freedom of emotional suffering that accompanies the world of being without a body. It is almost as good as they paint the pictures of heaven to be, but it is far more of a real feeling and a real life than the image of being with the angels.

"I am sure that you know that I have met with those who are my spiritual world advisors and I find them to be far more determined than what I imagined angels to be, and I have yet not seen any with wings. I was wondering for a time if I had not made the world known as heaven, but find that if there does exist another realm beyond this one that is closer to the image I was given of heaven, then I think that I would much prefer to make my home here."

The comment of hers about her spirit world advisors I have related to the concept of my guides. She never uses the term guides, but I lack a better definition of the term for spiritual advisors. For that matter, I lack a better definition of the concept of guides than spiritual advisors, for this is what they have been to me in this realm. It would seem that both perform the function of leading and prompting one to evaluate their lives in accordance with their lessons, with a view of growth for the individual in the area of spiritual understanding. Thus, I assume she is working closely with her "guides" by her statements.

Her comments about heaven are not the first time that I have encountered comments from those in the other world that does not align with the most prevalently held religious concepts of heaven. I have yet had a connection with anyone who has described the stereotypical angel with wings. There also seems to be a lack of any mention of thrones, harps, gates, or icons normally associated with the religious works of art seen around the world. I personally am curious what it is I will experience when I reach that realm. It will only be then that I can say for sure that such things exist or not. However, my research does lead me to believe that perhaps things are a tad bit different than what we in this world envision them to be.

She once again asks me if I am able to make a decision and, if not, what it would take for me to do so. I politely tell her that I have not exhausted my well of questions, and that by nature I am one who does not like to gamble on the unknown. I mention also that if this decision were just about me that I would be more prone to make one and not worry as much about the consequences. However, being a part of a family unit, my decision must be based upon far more factors than whether I am willing to jump off the cliff to see where I land. As it turned out, even with many more pages of transcript, it took me almost another year to integrate this whole concept into my being to feel secure enough to make this leap of faith. I will say that I admire her handling of this affair, for she never tried to unduly influence me or to badger me into doing this work. Her graciousness is part of why I did decide to go forward with this book project. I respect her waiting for me to make my decision and her faith that I would eventually see the need to write her words upon paper for distribution to any who would choose to judge for themselves the weight and meaning of her words.

CHAPTER 11

Soul Choices, Mutual Respect,
Mysterious Symbols

The dates of our transcripts now move forward into October of 1997. I had been ill with a lingering, but nonserious, illness and had not felt the energy to channel. When I regained my strength, I also regained my curiosity. I wanted to ask her about her feelings on the events of her life. However, as often happened with our conversations, and often happens with any conversation, we did not stick solely to my preplanned list of questions. I ask the question I want, but then it goes wherever it may from there.

I started this day of contact with her (October 7, 1997) by asking if she felt that meeting and marrying Charles had in anyway been preordained. In other words, had she come here to do what she ended up doing? Her answer is interesting and takes me to a question that had never occurred to me in any formal thought processes of my own.

> **** "I do not know if this is an answer, but the words of my advisors to me were that I had chosen this as a lesson for myself and the world of humanity and that I had consciously made the correct choices for this purpose. I do not understand if that means that I am able to make that

another work if I choose to come back, or if I have done all that I was supposed to do. I was told that not all who come to the world of physical get to do their intended purpose because they sometimes choose the wrong course while there. But then again, I was told that if they are working at all with their guidance systems they will find the forward momentum of their soul's desire.

"I cannot say that I knew any of this when I was there, but it did seem often that my life was going in a preordained fashion and I was only the former of what I thought of it. I was given the knowledge that if I had made the wrong choice then I would have still made the impact that I did, only in another way. It seems that if you have a will to do something then there is no way you can make a wrong choice for all things fall together for the good of the soul's reason to become physical.

"I was wondering if you have ever considered that we were meant to work together and that if I had chosen to make this work with another that you would have been able to make the connection with me anyway? I was told that I was scheduled to make you my form of voice and that you had chosen to be the voice of many for that to have been accomplished. I was wondering if you had given this any thought?"

Naturally, in my searching for a reason as to why she would talk to me, I had touched upon the thought that maybe it was meant to be. I didn't think too deeply about this, for it seemed to be too easy an answer for my intellect. I answered her and said no, that I really hadn't, except when a friend had suggested that I had been chosen, or recommended as it were, to Diana as a channel. There was no proof of a "referral" system within the world of spirit, so I did not dwell long on my friend's assertion. I did tell her that I had adopted the idea that when I had asked to speak to my guides about the reasoning for her young death that she had been looking for some way to speak her mind. I figured I had just been in the right "place" at the right time. I then ask her if she had any sound knowledge if it was meant to be that we work together.

**** "I have no real knowledge of this except for what my advisors have given me by way of inference. I seem to feel that they are working at making me aware of your feelings and thoughts quite often now, and this makes me think that I am to work with you for the purpose of something even greater than either one of us has been able to conceive."

R. "Could be. Trust me when I say that I never would have conceived of ever getting to speak to the Princess of Wales, even living. To think that I am speaking to her beyond her life is still pretty farfetched to me and I try not to think on it in any heavy, meaningful way because I don't think I can truly handle the magnitude of that thought. I have come to believe that you are who you represent yourself as being, and that alone is a major accomplishment for me....I still struggle with avoiding the urge to think that I am making this up and closing down on this so as to not have to face my insanity, but something feels right about what you say and how you say it, so I keep coming back for more....I would never have had the gall to speak to you had I met you in real life, so to think that I speak to you now is a little overwhelming."

**** "I do not know why you feel that I should be inclined to not speak to one who has so much to offer. I would have been impressed with you had we met in that life, and I am in awe of you and your abilities in this life. I was never one who could think that I was better than anyone, and so I had to make myself believe that people could be interested in what I had to say. It was the hardest thing for me to take on the responsibility of public speaking for I knew that everyone would be wondering why I was bothering with trying to make myself appear intelligent. I used to cry thinking that I would embarrass myself and it took many people a long time to convince me that I had something worthwhile to say. I understand your opinion of yourself, and I think that this is also another reason that we have hit it off so famously. I recognize the feelings within you and you in me.

"I was also able to feel your thinking that I would never be speaking to one so far beneath me. I wanted you to know that if I ever could have, I would have vastly enjoyed you as a close friend while undergoing the life that I had led. I was always hoping to make another friend and that was very hard for me in my position. It was not that I did not have the opportunity; it was that I could never feel that they wanted to be my friend for who I was and not who I made myself appear to be....I think that if my work does not go as I have planned, that you can rest assured that I would still seek you out simply for the pleasure of your company. There is something between us that is more important than your abilities and my feelings of isolation. It is what feels like true respect to me and that is a gift that is valued in any world."

She was correct. I had come to respect her more for who I experienced in her words and feelings than I would ever have done simply because of her position. Her position while living was indeed one worthy of respect, but not on such an internal level as I felt through working with her. I would have shown her respect had I met her in life, but the depth of feeling respect that I had come to know can only be borne of getting to know someone on an intimate level.

I thanked her for these kind words. They had made me once again feel humble, mixed with elation. Her thoughtfulness in her dealings with me became an impetus for me to want to work with her words and allow her the avenue of a voice into this world that she had the desire to reach, even after death. Had she not been so caring, gracious, and patient, I cannot say that I would have felt the same way about laying myself on the line for her. I found that I could not walk away and feel that I had turned my back on my newfound friend.

The next question I had for her concerned her statement about the other car and the decals. I asked her about the writing on the other car and asked her to describe it to me so that I might try and get a visual image.

**** "I was able to see that it was of symbols and made little sense to me. It seemed to be of the Greek symbols, and yet I did not recognize any of them. There was a star that encircled the emblems and another one at the right-hand corner. If I had to guess I would think that it was of Middle Eastern origin, or perhaps one of the countries that uses symbols to make the words....It seemed to be peeling off the windshield. I think it was an old sticker that had been for another country and had been forgotten.

"I will remember this as being the thing that made me realize that they were not with the photographers, because the photographers always have some form of press sticker if they work for an organized business. The ones who do not work for these companies may or may not have a sticker denoting that they are with the press. I was afraid that the photographers would be crushed if they tried to surround us, so I made the driver go faster. When the bodyguard gave him the command to keep them behind us, I think he knew too that they were not only seeking photographs."

R. "I think you may already know this, but the bodyguard seems to have no recollection of the chase or the accident. I was very disappointed with this news. I had hoped he could vouch for what you had told me. You know me and my wanting proof, even if only for myself."

**** "I know that he does not remember, but I think that he will. I was given the advice that his memory will return, but they may not release what he says to the police when he does remember the events....I fear for his well-being if he releases this to the wrong persons. I hope for his sake that he does not remember the accident, but I hope he remembers the car. I can only advise you to wait and see what happens, but remember that if he does remember, the police may not release the details if they are to further investigate this affair. I am hoping that they do not. It would only further my feelings of guilt if they were to make him suffer again for my sake."

"I am now able to remember most of my former life and I think that it is good to review this from time to time. It keeps me grounded to the fact that I was a human and that I did exist in a physical form. I am told that if you are here for many seasons that the former things pass out of your awareness. I do not wish for this to be the case and so welcome the contact with those who

can help me remember the gift of physical life.
Good day and good night."

I spent much time debating what to do with this information concerning the car and the emblems. I knew that it might well be valid and of some help to the investigators if this were the case. However, I did not know how to begin to contact those who would need this and lacked the courage to step forward and say that I had this information. There was no proof that anything I had recorded was accurate, and I had not yet made my determination to go public. Even now, I can only hope that this information may have some validity and if so that it can help those who can make use of it.

CHAPTER 12

Ironies, Harsh Words, Reformation

Diana, as I came to see her through our conversations, had a sense of humor that often took the form of taking things and putting a spin on them that indeed did give a humorous twist. I had always enjoyed ironic humor myself but found her views funnier than what I myself had been able to see out of this entire situation. She did wonders for me by looking at this tragedy through the lens of humor.

R. "I was wondering, Diana, if you had considered that the men who followed you were after Dodi rather than you? If these were of Middle Eastern origin, as you have supposed, then I think that it could have been something to do with him and his family."

**** "I am not going to be able to make this my theory because I feel very strongly that it was me that they wanted to halt. I knew there were people who resented the time that I spent with my work and that there were factions that felt I was purposely forging ahead with my work only to make the royals and the other aristocracies look and feel inadequate with their own deeds for humanity. My work was treading on tender toes. I was never afraid that they would try to cease my work with the use of violence, but there was feeling that they would want to discredit me. I was always wondering when the other shoe would drop, and I guess I now know that it was not a shoe but rather a form of boot.

"There could not be anything that would make me think that the ones who were responsible for this were going after Dodi, or as a retaliation towards his family. I only knew them to be good and kind people, and it seems that is why I cannot imagine that they were the targets. I think that if the real truth were known, it was never initially intended to make me die, only to scare me into quitting my work, but when the accident did happen they knew that I would be silenced. I was hoping that they would see that if they had not killed me then there would not have been the focus upon my good works that became so common during my death and internment.

"I was going to say that I had been given over to smiles about the irony of that, except since I do not have a mouth, I do not know exactly how to express it. I was wondering if you had given any thought to the fact that if they were only trying to scare me, then they are now the ones who are scared? I think this funny. I was wondering if you could make me feel your feelings on this? I would love to experience the feelings that you have upon the many ironies that seem to present themselves to us when we review this whole business. It seems to get funnier and funnier to me....I was wondering if you could also share your thoughts with me on why you are so serious with this whole thing. I want to make you see that I am not unhappy that the accident occurred, and that I can even laugh about the quirks and ironies that have presented themselves to me. Try to lighten up your view of this situation and give me your sense of humor."

I suppose that my sense of sadness and the sense of awe over this ability to speak to her had turned me into a very serious "reporter." I usually do have a good sense of humor, but had not yet felt comfortable with presenting jokes to her. I told her that I felt that since she was the one who had died I should be respectful, as I had always been taught to be at funerals. But, at her bidding, I joined into the game of finding the ironies that could make us "smile." I commented on the fact that if they had wanted her silenced then they had made a "grave" error. Her death gave her more clout with her good works than perhaps if she had worked behind the scenes for another forty years. I also said that if the photographers were the ones responsible, as the news reports had first led us to believe, then they had fried themselves also. "You always made good copy and much money was made by dogging you to death (no pun intended!). They killed the goose that laid the golden egg, and now they are probably crying in their photo developing solvent." Since the time of that comment, the photographers have been cleared of this blemish, and I therefore apologize for having used them in this attempt at humor.

I then said that I was glad she could feel good about the situation and find humor. I asked her about her feelings about the way the "kingdom" had responded to her death and their attempts to have the queen and the prince show more emotion with her death.

    **** "I had not thought of it that way, but yes, it does show me another facet of the humor and feelings that if they want to lead then they had better remember the feelings of the people. I think it ironic that some of them had to keep their own feelings about me and my work stuffed inside and pretend that they were truly grieving for me. I was so overwhelmed with the pretense that I gave myself the giggles....I felt rather sorry for the queen as I was truly fond of this woman on one level and hated to see her being caught up in the feelings that the crowd had for the queen and the prince.

"I truly tried to hold no animosity towards him because he is my children's father, yet I seemed to always come back to the fact that he was sometimes an insufferable pig and a fool, though we had found camaraderie after the divorce. I was so well loved by the world and so often well despised by my own husband....If I could do that life over, I would never let him get away with the affair for so long, but the others were the ones who made me keep my silence. I should have walked out the minute I knew...and given him the best view of my backside that I could have. He was a fool to make it such a travesty, for I knew that I held more power with the masses than he did. I was not going to use that, except to make him eat his words to me that he was what had made me who I was and he could make me be what he wanted me to be. I think he has seen the light of that foolish statement and if I have anything to do with it, he will make those words my final glory. I want him to realize that to feel that you own another person because you have the power of a country is not only foolish, but the epitome of grandiosity.

"There will be a reformation within my country of birth, and he will begin to see that to feel the power over anyone is to lose that power. He needs to know that all are created equal, even if you are born into the most well-known monarchy and have the power of governing the masses.

He will realize this when his son comes to power and he sees for himself that to rule with love and humility is the real power of having people love you back.

"The masses have already cried for his son to be ruler, and I only hope that William can be the man that I know him to be. I regret having to leave my sons to the hands of the monarchy, but again I am told that is the purpose that they chose to be who they came to be. I will await the power that my son has to be the people's king and then I will know that I am ready to retire from the world of physical and feel free to move forward with my next choice of lessons, and maybe even my own next physical life.

"I was wondering if you have given any thought to making this a memorial to me when the time comes. I am wanting to discuss this with you, and if you are of agreement, then we shall consider this the final thoughts of the fairy-tale princess. I will utilize others for my work also, but the greatest bulk of my personal thoughts and memories I will hold in reserve for you. I will want no other to represent me on such a personal level for I think that you have the feelings that I need for this to be the final will and testament of myself. I can only hope that you can find it in your heart to make this a consideration and let me speak to you of my deepest thoughts and wishes for my personal life....I am of deep gratitude with you for the format of making myself known and having the freedom of expression."

The words of Diana sometimes pull no punches with how she really felt. While this is good for her to have been so open with me, and they are perhaps no more or less candid views than she might have shared with others, it was part of what gave me pause about doing this project. I had to wrestle with the choice as to whether I wanted to report these words as received or do some heavy editing so as to not offend someone. However, as I wrangled with the decision to start this book, it became clear to me that if I were to do it at all, then I would need to print it as I received it. The entire book was to be about her words—and except for a few things that I have with-held for various reasons—these are the words as they were given to me. These views belong to her, are a part of her psyche, and it is not my role to buffer them or to wrap the punches in swaddling clothes. Thus, you get them as they were delivered, and I find I am not in a position to defend or deny them. I am just the secretary taking dictation and delivering the letter to the intended recipients.

CHAPTER 13

Rivalry, Solace, Life's Tapestry

The next set of questions, delivered on October 14, 1997, to Diana yielded yet another conversation loaded with some weighty statements. I asked her to tell me about the business with Camilla, her supposed "appearance" to someone, and why she had finally given up on her marriage. Here is her answer to two of the three questions:

> **** "I will approach this with the wit and wisdom of the ones who have been giving me my lessons over here. I was once a future queen, but I felt more the fugitive. I felt the burden of my position very heavily and I think that this was a grand lesson to me. I was never a rival to Camilla; she was a rival to me and my future happiness. I gave her the gift of knowing that I knew about her and Charles, but that was of no great concern for her. He had asked her if I should be the one he should wed, and she gave her consent. It was well known that they were an item, and that as long as he and she were discreet there would be little, if any, ramifications for them continuing their friendship.

"I was a sacrificial virgin for the masses and the throne's continuation. I was never intended to be the one who gave the masses their feelings of hope and inspiration, only their heirs. I was not intended to be the public figure that I became, and when the media fell in love with the fairy-tale princess, there was great consternation on the part of the lovers who wanted to use me as window dressing to keep their affair secret and alive. I was not the little mouse that Camilla thought me to be, and when I roared, she became even more obsessed with making me the villain in this sordid affair.

"I was to be the virginal little wife who pined for her husband's affections and suffered in silence. The ones who gave me the advice that all men will have their dalliances and all women must put up with this as a matter of due course did not want me to make this affair public knowledge. It was said that if I did so that I would bring reproach upon the throne and the masses would retaliate with hatred for me for being so feeble-minded as to let this become a factor of reproach upon the great and omnipotent prince of Wales.

"I was of the frame of mind that if I could make this work then he would eventually lose interest in this older woman and give me the love that I had reserved for him back to me. I was wrong, and even bearing his children did not endear him to me, and so I suffered in silence and agony as long as I could endure. When the tapes (his, hers?) became public knowledge, I felt there was no longer any reason for this charade to go on, so I began to plan my out of the fairy-tale kingdom.

"I forgave him the infidelity, you see, for it was not he who wanted to marry me, but the future of the kingdom that had to be his first priority. I cannot forgo the urge to make this an issue, so please bear with me for this next statement. I was a pawn in the world of the kings and the queens, but the future of the kingdom was never in danger. It was the future of the queen's house that was in danger, for if there were no heir through her elder son, then the throne would have went to the heir of the younger son or even to another lineage. I was one who wanted to do what was right, but not at the price of the future of the kingdom. I gave birth to my sons with the knowledge that they would be heirs, and this seemed good to me at the time. I was a very loyal subject to the throne and felt it my duty to do as bidden. I wanted to be the mother of the future king and gave myself over to the fairy tale long enough to produce the required heirs.

"I was astounded when the future king announced that since we had the heir and a spare that he would no longer choose to sleep with me, and that I was able to go my separate way. I began then to seek the solace that another man might offer me, and I found the experience quite rewarding. I have now found when one is inexperienced, there is a great deal that one does not know. I had considered being made love to a form of requirement, but then I knew the sheer joy of wanting to be made love to. I had never known a master craftsman in the subject until I began interviewing replacements, and I fell hard for the one who made me see the glory and the power of the flesh. I was foolish enough to think that this man would feel the same thing for me, and again I made the mistake of living in the land of make-believe. What seemed to me proof of love was for him only the proof that I could be had. It was a time of great growth as a woman to realize that one does not need love to experience ecstasy. I am now well versed on the format that when one does feel love there may be physical sensation, but if there is truly love then there is a joy to be had with the flesh that cannot be denied.

"I gave myself to the men that I did to prove that I was desirable and that I could make him jealous. It seemed to work only for his benefit. The more I gave myself over to the pleasures of the flesh, the more he could deny his guilt and his own infidelities. There was a tracking of my activities to ensure that I was in no danger of making a mistake that could endanger his own jollies, but beyond that I never felt that he cared if I was with other men.

"I grew depressed and despondent over my life with each passing affair, and I was glad that the affairs were finally brought to the forefront. I began to know then that I would be leaving the kingdom of the toad, and that I would walk away with my head held high. I assessed what I could do to ensure the future of my children, and I made the plans with infinite care. I was well advised to seek the public eye and to remain a central figure within the kingdom, but that meant that I needed to make myself over into the image that was of vulnerability and strength. I needed to make my exit with as little disgrace as possible if I was to be a figure that would endure, and so I chose to make myself over into the image that they had fought so hard to have me suppress.

I began to let the kingdom see me as a person and not as a princess on a pedestal.

"I began to use the media to my advantage instead of my destruction. I made sure that if I was photographed it was with those who would best make use of my presence and my desires for reform for those who have no power and prestige. I began to use the power of my station to (highlight, expose, convey? This word was missing from my transcript.) the plight of the needy and the ailing. I did it all to make my exit out of the kingdom mean more than my life in that same kingdom. I felt the urge to forgo the routine of having myself be the fairy-tale princess, and yet I knew that this was the role for which I must aim if I were to leave and do any good for the people who needed someone from the royal family to make the changes that were needed within the Kingdom. I grow tired of having to explain the concepts of why I chose to leave, so may we proceed with the other questions that you have for me?"

I also was growing tired at this point in the session. I never grew tired of speaking to her, but the chore of typing and concentrating hard enough to "hear" the information does takes a toll after an hour or so. I had spent many years building my stamina towards being able to channel for extended periods of time, but some of our sessions were going into overtime for my endurance. However, I did ask another question and thankfully the answer was short.

R. "There was an interview that you gave to someone for a book. I can't recall his name, but what do you say about this? (I now know his name is Andrew Morton. I had only remembered briefly hearing something about the book and the speculation of her hand in it at this point.) Why did you not tell me that there was another form of your life's story out there?"

****. "I can only say that when I spoke to the man known as Andrew, I was not aware that it would be my last opportunity to make my life's history known to the world. I am sure that he has utilized this collective to great benefit, but this was not my intention when we spoke. I wanted him to do this book and give the world some of the truth of my life, but I never felt that it would be the end story to that life. I am now giving you this so as to do a summation with my entire life and the reasons that I continue to care for the world of physical. I am working with you for the further clearing of the muddle that my life had become and the purposes that I have firmly in mind on what I hope to see accomplished with, and despite, my death. It is a far greater thing to make this a forum for my words than those that I had given at that time because it is now truly the final words of the fairy-tale princess. I will speak to no other of these very private issues and will release no other statements through another on why I did what I chose to do. It begins with him but may end with you.

"There will be a blending between what he has and what you will be given if you are of patience to make the journey with me through most of my ramblings. I will give to you those things that I have not given to him, and he will have that which we shall not speak of. Go with your own instincts of what is of value for you to read and to know while speaking to me, for it will make no difference in the end what you have read elsewhere, or what you have heard. There

will be enough of what I have given you to make
the tapestry all come together with great success
and great beauty of form. I will make this known
to you at some future date, so do not worry with
this at this point. I am confident with your skills
and you should be also. Believe in yourself."

We did not, unfortunately, cover the information concerning
her statement made earlier about having made an attempted "appearance" to someone. I had forgotten that I had even asked the question
initially in light of her extended response about her marriage and the
events contributing to her decision to leave. It was not until review-
ing the material several months later that I realized I had not pressed
her again with this question.

There is a statement in this fragment of our dialogue that I have
never been able to understand. It concerns the future of the queen's
house. It seems that she was under the impression that if the throne
went to the heir of the younger son that it would adversely affect the
structure of something she termed "the queen's house." I have as yet
found any information that clarifies this for me, and I know that
others may have the same puzzlement over this statement as I. I have
begun to consider that perhaps it is something of a personal wanting,
or "internal goal," and not anything related to the actual protocol of
lineage succession. I offer this weakly as a very unfounded theory.
In other words, my best guess at what this could mean. My research
leaves me no wiser.

My last question to her stemmed from the fact that I had been
made aware of the existence of a book that had covered her life. I had
been told that she had helped to write this story and was very curious why she had not told me this herself. I had been told the name
of the author, but at the time of the session could not remember it.
As I said much earlier in this book, I actually did not get to read
this author's work until the commemorative edition given to me in
August of 1998. It may seem odd to some of you that I did not rush
out to buy this book written about her life, but I did not want the
interference of what I read to mingle with what I was receiving. I did

not want what I read to bias what I "heard." I tried very hard during the most active part of my channeling of her words to keep myself from unduly reading or watching an abundance of things about her.

It was, of course, impossible to avoid all things associated with her or her life during the time immediately following her death. It would be wrong of me to say that I did not glean some things from the news or the wealth of written material bombarding the world. (It was not feasible for me to go live on a remote island during this time!) My idea was to limit what I could, trying to work with my sessions with her as my main source of knowledge. I found myself in a dilemma, however, because I needed to monitor whether what I had matched any facts. Therefore, I enlisted the aid of some friends who were privy to my "secret" and were reading the transcripts to keep their eyes and ears tuned to the data coming out and let me know if we had any matches. This was not only an attempt at purity of channeled information, but also to prove to myself that I was not making this up. Only those who channel, or have intimate knowledge of someone who does, may understand the thought processes that makes someone question themselves endlessly, and keeps them striving to prove it to themselves even more so than to others.

CHAPTER 14

Emotional Equivalence, Higher
Flames, Frivolity

Each session with Diana led me further and further into what
seemed to me to become a friendship. It was an odd concept
to think that I could feel the feelings that I was experiencing
for someone I had never met, would never see face-to-face, and was
not even physical. However, in hindsight, I have heard many people
express this same concept about those people that they meet through
Internet access from all over the world. It would seem that channeling is not that different at its core than using the Internet to communicate. Both involve speaking to those we have not yet met, and
may never meet, but the essence of their being is given to us through
their words and the choosing of them. One is more acceptable only
because there is a tangible piece of technology to link the two minds,
but both involve the linking of minds for expression and sharing of
information.

Her willingness to communicate with me and offer such intimate truths, perspectives, and humor had worked its charm on me
as surely as if I had met a new person at work, the gym, or the mall
who would become a good friend of mine. Actually, during this time,
I was spending more time with her than any of my "real" friends. I
was rewarded time and again with a wonderful feeling of happiness

and eagerness for our conversations, just as if she had been down the street and was someone I really cared to spend time with.

This next session is from mid-October 1997. I approached her again with a question that tied in with the previous session.

R. Tell me some more about your life and the feelings that you had while here. Why do you feel that Camilla had such a hold upon your husband?

**** "I am growing tired of the theme of Camilla and her interference with my life. I know now that I was intended to make the choice to have married the prince, but that I was to never know marital bliss for that would have greatly hampered my efforts of helping those who were in pain. To more fully empathize with those who were feeling aloneness and despair, I had to be there in an emotional equivalent. I was meant to know the joys of helping others, but it was only through my own pain and feelings of rejection that I could do that which I had been of intent to do.

"I think that my husband was of being so obsessed with Camilla for she was a temptress of the highest sort. She made sure that if he strayed too far afield that she reeled him back in with promise of even more of her charms. I think that they had met young and it was she who had introduced him to the pleasures of the flesh. I think she was quite capable of keeping him in reign for he was not one who could easily make the distinction of what was real and what was being given to him for the purpose of manipulating him with his own desires. I feel certain that if he had given me only half of the interest that he had for her, our lives together would have been vastly different. I am now finished with this entire affair and wish to put that part behind me.

"I will now give you the reasons that I have come forward to those of you who can and do receive me. I wanted to make this another session where we delve into the reason why I feel the need to continue with the realm of physical existence. I have been made aware of the many things that can and do work with the realm of spiritual thought, and I feel that if there is not a reformation in my country and the world at large there will exist many more decades of moral turpitude and decay. There needs to be a focusing of the greater good rather than the prevailing attitude of seeking only what behooves the immediate needs of the family. I was one who gave up on getting anything out of the family that I was born or wed into but began to research into the world as a whole as a family that needed to become my home. I was not happy as a child and I feel that if I had worked with the same principles of making my family feel what I have with the entire world, then there would have been a reformation within my own family unit.

"What the lessons of my childhood taught me were that if one is not happy with the world, then one cannot be happy with the immediate family. My mother grew disenchanted with the family life as she knew it to be and went out with the idea of reconstructing her life in another area. There was much satisfaction for her in this, except for her to have accomplished this she had to make the rest of the family readjust their roles as well. It seemed to me to be the epitome of self-ishness to make others pay the price of your own personal happiness, and I think this was when

I discovered the truth that to make one's self happy at the price of others was not the best way to proceed.

"As I became the fairy-tale princess, I took this lesson with me to the altar. I knew then that to have this opportunity was a lifetime of lessons for those who have no hope. I was never able to explain this to anyone else, but I felt the need to share what I thought of as my great fortune and blessing to become the princess of the greatest kingdom to ever exist. I realized that if a fairy-tale princess could be made from a lonely, shy, gawkish young girl, then the world could be transformed into the beautiful place that had been intended by the Creator of all men. I felt the urge to share what I had with those less fortunate and would have done so if I had been able to make the transition within myself to be the force that I craved to be. I wanted from the first to make the world a greater place but the restrictions that were placed upon me by the true powers would have none of it. They meant for me to only be the mother to the heirs and an obedient wife to the future king. I was not yet strong enough to have found my own inner strength about who I was and who I could be to refute their efforts at making me into what they saw me to be. I fought long and well, I might add, to become the woman that I did and I paid the price in personal happiness. I was careful to make this work of undoing what they had started bear witness to my own efforts of being the one who could rise above fame and power and wealth to truly care for those who were the ones who needed the media exposure. I never meant for this to make the world another battleground for the wealthy versus the poor, but I sometimes feel that if I had not died then that would have eventually been the outcome."

Diana Red Cross Water Color © McMahon 2002

R. "Can you explain that statement?"

**** "I am going to say this and perhaps this will clear that provocative statement. I wanted the world to see me doing what all of wealth and nobility should do with their assets and freedom of time. I meant for this to be a role model for the world to see that those who have should be those who give. Yet it seemed that when the media carried images of me to the world doing what I felt needed to be done, I became a sore spot for those who have but do not wish to share. I made the forefront of many news stories and yet it seemed the ones who gave were the ones who had the least. I was saddened by the news to me that there were those who had it to give but wanted only for me to take a backseat with my own activities

so as to not create an unfavorable comparison.
The battle lines were being drawn, not by the
ones without, but by the ones with the means
to help end world suffering. I would not want
the ones without to make the mistake of giving
while those with sat idly by and made no move to
help those who had taken up the fight on world
poverty, sickness, and injustice. I made the battle
begin to heat up and I felt the desire to make the
flames get hotter and higher for those who could
help but chose not to. I was well aware of the intimated threats given to me by several sources, yet
I had no intention of being the shy little princess
who went back to the land of make-believe that
all was right in the world. I had intended after
my marriage to Dodi to make the flames reach
a feverish pitch and with his help and backing
would make the battle lines disappear by means
of guilt laid at the feet of the guilty.

"There were those who would swear that I
intended to marry Dodi with the intent of furthering my own security, and this is not so far
from the truth. I did not intend, however, to make
the marriage for solely the creature comforts for
my children and myself. I was working with him
for the furthering of my charitable works and
the security that he could offer the children and
I from the backlash that would ensue when the
flames reached the point of true cleansing of the
greed that would burn up within these flames.

"Dodi was a generous man who felt, as I
did, that there could be many great things accomplished if the world at large would assume that if
we have the homeless, the dying, and the sick,
that we are responsible for those conditions. He
had remarked that if he had enough funds on his

own, he would take each child and give them a pony to see the expression on their faces and to hear their laughter. I loved him for his generosity and spirit of love for others. He was a fair and kind man. We would have accomplished many great things together. He knew how to love and how to share joy and laughter.

"I am most despondent over the fact that he too was taken in the crash, for if he had survived he would have made an effort at making our dreams come true without me. I guess that to have been there without me would not have had the same impact as the tragedy that did transpire. I must assume that all has worked according to the higher plan to awaken the world through the loss of all of us. I grieve for the fact that I can no longer work with the world directly, but this is why I have made the determination to use the abilities of those such as yourself to further the work that was so dear to my heart.

"I guess that I should say soul, for I no longer have a heart with which to feel this desire. As you can see, I am still adjusting to not having the physical body to make my thoughts seem coherent with my true state of being. There are many examples that I have thought of with this, and here are but a few. I can no longer feel anything, work my bum off or have it chewed out, make love rather than be love, or give myself a shot in the arm. I think I amuse myself in some funny ways, don't you agree?"

R. "Quite cute, I think. How about these? You can no longer drop to your knees, stick your foot in your mouth, give a helping hand, take it on the chin, belly up to the bar, have a knee-jerk reaction, run yourself ragged, or stick your nose into anybody's business. Thought of those?"

**** "I am quite impressed with your spirit of joining in. I had thought of some of those but will add the others to my list of humorous things that I can no longer do. There is quite a lot of humor with being dead if people would lighten up on the subject and give in to their playful natures. I was often afraid that I would laugh at funerals for I often saw the most perverse humor sometimes. I am going to let you retire now with this session and thank you again for the company and the frivolity that you afford me. I am going to speak to you next on why we must make this work available...There will be another lesson in there for you about why the world perceives only that which can be proven and why they must make the change over into believing the world of nonphysical does exist. Until then, take care that you leave nothing for yourself that you do not wish to be remembered for. It makes a mark every time you use another without the benefit of giving something in return. I do not intend this as an omen, but it would do well for all to make this discovery while they have time to correct the marks that are being made by them."

Our fall into giddy humor and goofiness was quite natural, and evidence to me that we had established a rapport that was feeling free and easy with us both. Her ability to make light of the situation she found herself in has done much to alter my view of the sadness and morbidity that we assign death. While it is true for us left behind that we are often sad and grief-stricken, it has made me aware that it may be much less so for those who find themselves in the condition known as dead. I have, as yet, not had contact with any from that side of consciousness that lament and carry on about being the dead with equal zeal as those left behind to mourn for them. There is a sadness about not being with those loved ones, but it seems that they have a much greater ability to tune into us in this world than we do to them. Thus, it seems to them that the finality of never seeing their loved ones again is much less a burden to them than for those in our world who do not believe that communication is only a thought away.

The next conversation that I had with her was not found on my computer the next day when I returned to edit it. I can only assume that I made the mistake of turning off the computer without hitting the save button. The discovery of this error hit me with great fear. It seemed a great mistake to not record a session with her, and try as hard as I could, I could not accurately remember what we had discussed. I thought that she would be angry. I felt great guilt over not having saved her words, and I was even hesitant in contacting her to tell her what I had done. (As if she might not already know?) But it seemed only right to admit to my blunder and apologize profusely. Once again, I had underestimated the graciousness of this being.

> ****. I am able to make this a trivial thing in my long-range goals, so why should we regress when we can move forward? I was only explaining why I would choose to make myself known and this is going to be self-evident when the deed has been accomplished. Let us resume our conversation from the point where we were and not cry over lost words."
>
> R. "Thank you for being so gracious and we can begin the next of your transmissions now."
>
> **** "I have been more than responsible for many of the mistakes that you will find yourself making with this assignment, so do not feel that I am being unduly gracious....I have given you some erroneous information because I did not come to this assignment well prepared for the questions that you would ask. I have also had

some memory problems with those things of your world that did not affect me emotionally, so if anyone should bear the brunt of this work being anything less than it could have been, it will rest with me. I have no fear that you will know that I have spoken with great clarity on these subjects that have given me the most emotional forms of memory, but then there are those things that I must work at recalling.

"I am going now to tell you of why we must work at getting this information out to the world before the full year of my death. It is going to be human nature for the masses to commemorate the anniversary of my death. If there is any indication that I have been able to speak or communicate with those of your world, it will heighten the awareness of this if it has transpired before I have become another one of those lost souls in the minds of the public who believe, as I did, that there is only one of two places to go after you have died.

"I am going to be working with you and the one who will break the ground for the completion of my own memorial. I will then proceed to work with another who will make the final gift of making the words that you and he have delivered seem to be of greatest value.

"I would request that you keep our correspondence a secret except for the chosen few who are of now being aware of it. I want this to work with the greatest of timing and do not want to risk a premature leak to the people who may not work at this for the highest of reasons. I have met and made acquaintances with many of the world of the media. There are a few who I find to be of great integrity, but the majority do not care for the feelings of the ones that they cover, or their own consciences on how to get what they are after.…It would also escalate the unnecessary tabloid frenzy that I so greatly want to avoid until the other that I work with may be prepared for his role. I am going to reveal to each of you the secrets of the fairy-tale princess and the motivations of why she remains concerned for the world of her children.

"I was once cast upon the waters of being bolted into infamy and would desire this for no one. Our gift of working as we have been given the grace to do is for our mutual benefit, not for the benefit of the hounds who would tear asunder the flesh of those they pursue. We may avoid much of this if the approach is well coordinated and given when all are of sufficient preparation."

Her response put me at ease with my mistake, but I began to worry over her comments about errors in what I had. I came to the conclusion that, as she had said, there was enough accurate information that would confirm her presence with me that I decided to not let it worry me overly much. I decided to forge ahead and not belabor the past statements that might be less than what they could have been. She didn't seem too concerned, and it was her ball game, so to speak, so why work myself into a frenzy?

CHAPTER 15

Working with Others,
Continuing Education, Soul Evolution

Her previous comments about making this available to the world before the anniversary of her death is obviously not what happened. I was not prepared to rush into this. There was much work that needed to be done within me to make a decision to get involved and to assume that I could write this down and present it to the world. I needed the time and distance of not working with her to objectively come to a conclusion on how I felt about this material. It seemed, in the long run, to not make a difference to her that this first established deadline was not met. In later sessions, some almost a year after her death, she still wanted the same result, just now it would be at a time when I was more capable of thinking about it doing it with emotional and mental equilibrium restored and a firm idea that this was the right thing to do.

The knowledge that she had said that she would work with another, or others, was part of what kept me from moving ahead. At some point, she had mentioned that this one might take the lead with announcing that they had spoken to her, so I waited. In later sessions, there will be more coverage of this aspect and why I waited. If there has been another, I am unaware of it at this moment, but that does not mean that it is not so. Perhaps he or she has, and is, suffering the same fear that I have known about making something like this public. If there are others, then my jump into the unknown might well help them to leap forward with faith also.

Now let us go back to her words of this conversation on October 22, 1997.

**** "I am now going to address why I am working with the realm of spirit and the realm of form to make the contributions that I have begun. I was given the opportunity to live in a world that had fallen far from the grace of highest ideals. I saw more of the life of the well-established than most, and yet I cannot assuage my guilt over the ones who never had an opportunity for the basics in life. I was never one who felt that just because I was from one given family that I had any more to offer than another from a less established bloodline. I have met some very great people in the most humbling of circumstances, and it is this that has convinced me that to do without is not a sin, but to have and not do with is.

"I am greatly wanting to make this statement for the sake of my son's future reign as king, and his brother's role as prince. It will do well for them to know that if I can reach them, then they can reach those that they have not yet seen. It is a cloistered environment that they live in, and yet I have made them aware of the wisdom that not all are of the same level of understanding, comfort, and grace that they share because of the circumstances of their birth. I hope to show them, more than anyone else, that to have is a duty to work with those who do not.

"I am orchestrating this entire project, not solely for the effect that it will have upon the lives of the ones in need, but also for the lives of those who I had given life to. I am still their mother in my thoughts and I feel the need to continue the education that I had found most important for them. This will, in and of itself, help the kingdom, for I was the bearer of the future king. As the mother of a ruler within the world of form, I can do no less than to oversee the education of my son for the betterment of the world at large, and his own well-being upon the realm of spirit. It is his destiny and I am going to fulfill my part of it with all that I have.

"It will suffice to say that if I can make this idea work, then I have done what I can to make a difference upon that world and I will feel that I am deserving of the next step within my soul's evolution. I am not intentionally holding back this evolution, for if I can accomplish this magnitude of service, then I will have evolved the spirit of community service and greater good for all that is the foundation of the world of spirit. I am also going to state that if we are capable of doing this as a unit, then the level of service that each of you have offered will also be an evolution for the good of your soul's higher intent to make you a fountainhead of God's will and love.

"This, I am told, is the greater reason that the soul leaves the spiritual realm at all and occupies the realm of form. It is for service and knowledge of God's love for all that the soul chooses to make a contribution to the world of form and why the soul must sometimes bear great sufferings in order to receive the love from another source.

"I am going to close this session and will next speak of the magnitude that this will have upon the world's ideologies of what the world of spirit is, and why it is so misunderstood in that world. It will be a large undertaking, so be prepared for a lengthy session when we next meet. I am your friend and will await your time with me. Good day to you and may you find the will to keep this in perspective as you have been so able to do. It is an amazement to me that you can so well believe this and can be within two worlds with such clarity and precision, and yet not lose the focus of that world. I am your student with this, and a grateful one to be sure. Make this my last statement for today."

How refreshing to know that one who had many material advantages handed to them at birth could feel, identify, and show such compassion for those who were not so privileged at the onset of life. I have often wondered if I, in the same situation of wealth and rank, would have been able to be so aware and open to the voids experienced by others. It has made me look at my own life, and while I have never had any abundance of wealth or status, I realize now how lucky I have been compared to some. Her grace, humility, and compassion seemed to be contagious, at least in my own mind. Perhaps we all need to see what she saw through those large cornflower blue eyes.

Her words about working still for the benefit of her sons and the lessons that she feels that are important to their futures strikes a chord in me as being the truth. Yes, it would seem that she has the welfare of others in their physical lives in mind, but her main concern is for her sons. Not only what may come in their lives while physical, but what the spiritual outcome from their actions may bring. A good mother would have this interest in her children, and I do believe that it may well extend beyond this world. Why should the bonds forged by love end at death, since the world of spirit (or heaven if you prefer), must be a realm of love? Most of our religious beliefs surround this key concept, and it may now well be the beginning of being proven as more contact with that world is established.

Her comments on soul evolution give rise to many thoughts. On a personal level, I do not doubt what she has said. It makes as much sense to me as anything I have heard elsewhere. There cannot be any proof of this, but I see this as the same as a lack of hard-core proof that God exists. There is no proof that can ease all minds, but the extrapolation and therefore the belief of most persons I know is that God does indeed exist. Is it so hard to believe that there is a purpose of the soul and that it seeks to fulfill it here in our world and the realm beyond? That we have an ability to care and strive for things after death? Well, for me in my life, it is not. Once upon a time I would have believed that speaking to anyone from the other side would not be possible. There was no proof that anyone could have offered me to convince me otherwise—not until I had the experience myself, and proof handed to me over and over again. In my life I have had to open my eyes, and my mind, very wide indeed. I sense that there are many other things that we do not fully know and understand about spiritual issues and may not ever have defined proof for. Thus, I keep my mind open and let it wrap around many things that I would have scoffed at or defended with religious dogma in my old state of narrow-minded existence. It seems that the wider the mind, the more that may enter.

CHAPTER 16

Monarchy, Forgiveness, Molding of a King

O ur next conversation on October 27, 1997, was a long one. It was a verbal monologue on her part, but the information was concise, almost as if she had prepared for this and had written a statement. I had trouble keeping up with the flow of words and was therefore not able to think of what she was saying as she spoke. I had to wait until the session ended to go back and read it to make sense of all that she had said to me.

This is quite often the case when the flow is strong and quick. It is too much to "hear," translate, type, and analyze all at once. When this happens, I dedicate my focus on getting the words typed well enough to know what was meant when I go back to edit. I leave the job of trying to understand it until such time as I go back to read it for editing. I am often amazed at what sense the transcripts do make when I have only recorded the words individually as they arrive without putting them together to see if they make a cohesive whole.

We will pick up into the meat of the session, as I have skipped over the greeting and the parts that have no depth to them. Since the session is a long one, this chapter shall be nothing more than her words from this point.

**** "I was given the advice by my advisors
that they want me to work with you on the pre-

sentation of this material as a form of giving the world another way of seeing the formation of a different society, one that may be ruled with a king and a queen without the benefit of the others being downtrodden. I am having difficulty explaining to you the wisdom that there is nothing wrong with the monarchy as a form of government, for you are of the world that left the reign of the former for the form of self-government. I am not trying to do away with the governmental form of monarchy, just the form of monarchy as it existed within my physical lifetime.

"I was not overly concerned about the wisdom of this when I was living, for there were always more pressing things for me to attend to. It was not the wisdom of the world to make the words of my physical life mean to them what the words would of necessity mean to them now that I am gone from their world. I was not allowed to express the disgust that I felt for those who would not share their great wealth with those who had nothing, and yet the world saw me as part of the problem. I cannot dismiss the fact that I did indeed live within the world of the upper established families, and therefore bear great burdens of guilt that I did not give as I have now come to believe that all should do. I was given great opportunities for freedoms that others can only dream of. Yet, I never felt that I could change the world I knew until after my divorce from the royal family. I had begun to use what I had left from the marriage to work at giving to those who needed and would have continued doing so if I had been there longer.

"I am not going to seek comfort in the fact that I did do some things to make the plight of the needy better. If I had been more fully awakened to the fact that all must give from what they have, I would have found other ways to make the contributions that I did give even greater. I am now settled upon a course that can help with this even after my physical life has faded from that world and will give this over to those who can manipulate this within your world of form.

"I am calling upon those of you who can and will work with me to be the voice and the eyes that I no longer possess, to make the changes that I had begun grow even more in intensity and depth. I was allowed to contact those of you who are in communication with me now for this purpose, and we shall make an excellent team if we are committed to each other and to the project of helping all who need those who can speak for them.

"I am given the advice that you are to speak for others, and this is as it should be. I am not entitled to be the sole preoccupation of the one who may help many and this is a great joy to me to know that you are going to use your wonderful skills for the betterment of many who need them. I am going to work with you for a defined period, then when you are able to speak to another, I will still be here if you wish to speak to me, but the weight of our correspondence will be finished.

"I am therefore eager to tell you of the many things that I hope to accomplish and how I have determined to do these things that must be done. I have given you the outline for the foundation that has been created in my name. There will be some further fine-tuning of this, but you have the main ideas and the thrust of what I expect this system to be like if I am to be the foundation's figurehead. I will also give you the knowledge that another will have these same guidelines so that there will be no mistaking these as a creation solely coming from you. I am aware that there will be much controversy over whether you have created these writings for the purpose of fame and fortune, so I will provide protection for you and the others by duplicating the contents of the material for the ones involved so that there can be a matching of the contents to see that it was given by the same hand to several sources. I will also give them the information about the car and the accident so that they too can verify what we have spoken of. I want no one to suffer undue persecution with this, and if it appears from several sources, then this may help with the naysayers who would accuse any of you as manufacturing this for personal gain.

"I am quite taken with the generosity of the media on my death and will make this statement to all of you who can receive my thoughts. I was hounded by the media at all cost and at all times, but I have come to realize it was part of the process to make me so well known to the world so that my purpose after my death could be accomplished. I am forgiving of the media now that I have ascertained that it was their destiny to do that which they did to help provide the groundwork for the destiny that I find myself having to accomplish. If I had not been so forced into becoming the fairy-tale princess, then I could not produce the impact that I did while living. Most certainly not what I will produce now that I have attained the gift of being who I know myself to be here in this realm. I am grateful now for those who spent the time and energy to make my life so focused into the public eye. I will give this same announcement to the other ones working with me. This shall prove also that I am speaking to all of you, for there would not be any who would think to make the story read that I had forgiven the media and the processes that made my public and private life there in the realm such hell.

"I will now proceed to describe the things that I hope to accomplish with my work with all of you. I hope to be made known to the world not only for the giving of gifts that may result to the needy from my foundation, but also for the procuring of the right atmosphere for the beginning of my son's reign as king. I wish to show the world that when one wants to rule, one must do so with the intent of making life better for those who are their subjects, and that to do otherwise is a travesty of their powers. My son will become king within a short enough time and this is why I have decided to make this attempt to correct what I can for the preparing of his reign. I want him to know that his mother is still concerned with the kingdom and its people. Even more important to me is for him to know that I still do want him to become the man he is and not be molded into the form of man that he and I despise. He will know that I have given him many lessons on why there is such a broad range of people who exist within one kingdom and he will know what we have discussed as being the way to solve that. I am concerned overly much with his education and I think that he will receive another one knowing that I do exist in another world and yet still care deeply for the world he inhabits.

"It should teach him that I am concerned not only for the English, but for the world as a whole. We had often discussed the fact that it was not about countries as much as it was about people, and I am glad that we had these discussions. We could never find a reason why there should ever be a land where there was not justice and civil rule over people, except for the injustices of those who ruled the country. He knew full well that there could never be another fall of the forces of injustice unless there was a greater force of the ones who were just and willing to make the dedication to eradicate the sources of injustice. He knew also that there would be a time when he would take the throne of one of the greatest countries and he would have to be a force for the issue of justice and integrity for his people to help work at eradicating the forces of injustices elsewhere.

"He is well prepared for this role. I can thankfully say that my years that I did have with him were not wasted, but rather productive on showing him the gifts that he possessed. I am content to allow him to make his decisions for I know what spirit and soul lay within my son's physical body. I am very proud to have been given the gift of helping him recognize his own greater potential. He will become an example to be reckoned with, and if I am able to help him from this realm, I must begin the process of creating a spirit of giving freely to those who need from those who have.

"This is my primary work, and yet if I can only accomplish one small thing from here, it would be to have them all realize that what you do while living will be held to you when you are of the world of spirit also. It is not a form of punishment, as I had been told, but rather a form of growing and reaching ever higher for the greater good of all that have been created within the world of physical form. It is a growing of the gift of God's love to the world of form and that it is a form of the entire world of spirit expanding as well. I have learned many things here, and of all the things that I have been made aware of, this is the most profound wisdom. I am hoping to pass this along by example, and by word, to my children and the world that they must inhabit for some time yet. I am aware that in this realm that they are not truly my children, but the gift of another choosing to come to the world of form as my children, but this does not stop me from making them a priority in my thoughts even now. If they have chosen to be the children of the fairy-tale princess, then they have chosen to be the bearers of the means to help with this work also.

"It is not that this will get accomplished by any one group of people, but there will be many who will help with this reformation for the world. I am not discussing just the reformation of the country that I knew, but the reformation of the world's whole view, person by person, until there is a balance in the favor of the ones who give being greater than those who receive. It will create a shift in the momentum of the world's thinking, and therefore the world's reality. May we all be successful with this endeavor and may we all feel the gift of being able to create the world as we see it should be.

"I will ask that you work with me for another short season and then we will meet again when you are of the ability to do so with regard to checking in on an old friend. I am quite capable of making this project get started without tying you up from being of service to others, so make your friends (guides) aware that I have been given the advice from my advisors to free you up for their next project with you.

"I have many things to orchestrate before this occurs, so do not be saddened over our lack of communication. I will always answer your call for communication; I will just not be working with you on more of this project shortly. It will suffice until there is a need for this to become public, so make use of your freedom of time from our endeavor to help the others who wait for those of our world to come through and receive their thoughts. It is not often that there can be such clear communication from this world to yours, so you will be in high demand I am told.

"I am now going to free you up for your own life and will make my presence known more fully to the other so he can feel my intent with his thoughts. I am humbly your greatest fan over here, and will always be your friend. This is not the end of a friendship, just the end of a few short chats about my wishes and desires. I will allow you to help others as you have helped me but would ask that you remember that within the next few months there will be much that needs to be done before we are to work together again. I might suggest that you align your life to take advantage of this free time, for when we are given the chance to go public with this information there will be little precious time of freedom. It will entail much work on your part and the part of the others, so be prepared.

"I am always your friend and you are always welcome here in my world. Thank you for these sessions, and I will await to hear from you again."

CHAPTER 17

~~~~~~~~~~~~~~~~

Three Convictions

Knowing that my conversations with Diana would be concluding, at least as far as receiving this type of material, did cause me some sadness, but I was ever hopeful that she meant what she said about staying in touch with me. Even though this material was riveting, it was not the only thing that I wanted from her. I had indeed become quite fond of who was represented here through these words and admired her thought processes. I wanted to maintain a friendship, even if we spoke not a word about anything we had covered already. I was hoping that her promise to stay in touch was not the standard brush-off. You know, as in the "Hey, I'll call you and we'll do lunch!" promise, which never materializes. Fortunately, I have spoken to her since, and she has indeed answered me. Of course, it has always been connected to the material, or the wrestling with the decision to do a book, but at least she was there!

The following conversation which occurred on November 11, 1997, was not actually the last one. However, after this one with her, I did get involved with some other projects that kept me occupied. Therefore, it was many months before I spoke to her again. There are four to six other conversations that we had in 1998, one of them culminating in the momentum for me to begin this book and holding some suggestions from her on the actual writing of it. However, we shall continue our forward chronological flow of transcripts to not to lose track of the timing value, and to not lose anything that might mean something to someone. I begin this conversation with her by asking for a few answers to some questions, but again it seemed that she had an agenda she wanted to present first. Here are her words:

> **** "I am going to speak first if that is of no great restriction to you or your patience. Our world here in the realm of spirit is one that works very closely with the world that you inhabit. It is not that we can always know what you and the others of the realm of physical are about, you understand, but rather we work with your energy essences to make the connection to your spiritual guidance systems. I am of the understanding that you have been given the work of working with another who has been slain, and I would recommend to you that you continue with this for the time that we are not together. I can well understand the feelings of one who has made the transition from your world to this world, and if she was killed with much violence, then there must be an even greater wanting to work with your world for the gift of making her wishes known. I am very greatly rewarded for my efforts to have contacted and connected with you. I can only wish this for all who have need of your services and would recommend you very highly if I am ever given the opportunity to do so.
>
> "I was once someone who was afraid to speak her mind, and now I find that I have no greater desire than to do precisely that. I am going to require your services again as we have discussed, but there is another matter that I feel we must cover. I am not wanting you to release this information until we have both agreed upon this, and if I have read you correctly, you will not

do what is not of greatest value to all involved. I am requesting that you do not give this to anyone, and that if I have not accomplished what I have set out to do, then we shall discuss the possibility of you making this a memorial to me in the form of a book. Are we of agreement that you will not give this to any one until I have had the opportunity to make the connection with these others that I have spoken of?

R." Yes. I am only considering this as a book if nothing happens in the next year or so. Even at that, I may never do it, but will ask your permission first. I feel gifted to have had the opportunity to make the connection to you, and as you have said, it seems that we are supposed to do this. If that is correct, there is some purpose to be served and we shall figure this out as we proceed. I am waiting for your lead with this project and you have no need to worry about me jumping the gun. I have enough to keep me busy, so rest assured that you shall have the final say. If I should disagree with you at some future point, then we will, as friends, work at a compromise. Good enough?"

**** "I am well relieved that you do not want to make this a book without my permission, and if the plans I have made do not follow through, then I may work with you for just that purpose. I am still wanting to make the world see that I have spoken to others also, so make this your gift to me that you do not work with this information in any way so as to place yourself in the media's eye as the sole receiver of my words. It is a protection for you also that I request this and would not wish for you to receive undue willfulness of the media. I am very well versed upon the media's relentlessness and would wish to spare you the greatest burden of that.

"I am now going to discuss the further morals and wisdoms that I want made to those who would make my name the figurehead for this vast amount of monies that has been accumulated due to my passing over. I am wishing that all who work for this foundation be of the highest character, and that all who are in the working force for this give their word and intent of honesty. I am not going to wish that they all be of my country, for I feel that if there is a blend of many there will be more of a wanting to make this money work for the whole world and its needy.

"I am also going to ask that if there is ever another work to be done in my name that the foundation oversee the financial aid that it gives to them. I want there to be uniformity of purpose and a reflection of the values that I hold as important for the betterment of all societies. I will establish a gift of my advice through one of the voices that I have chosen. If there be any dispute of what it is I am wanting, there can be a direct connection to me for the purpose of making a fair and impartial decision based upon how I wish my name to be represented.

"I was not one who ever got to give what I wanted to give, so if I can do so now, I see no reason for this not to be so. There is yet another matter of great importance to me to cover with this session and I will proceed with this shortly, so be prepared for another whim of mine to be given to you. I am not going to preside over the day-to-day running of the foundation, but I do request the right to make statements that I feel reflect the spirit that needs to be given in my name. There will be another session on this when we are making the world know of my presence, so for now we shall move to another topic.

"I am of great conviction that there needs to be a lessening of the social values attached to the monarchy and that is rather a broad statement of fact. I am going to break this down into three areas of my convictions, so be prepared to receive them as such. The first area is of greatest importance for the people of the kingdom. It is of no great value that they remain silent to the workings of the royal family and their moral convictions. By this I mean that when the royals are acting without the highest of morals, there should be an outcry from within the ranks of the people of the kingdom. I am aware of the irony that I play into by making this statement, for I was one who had acted with less than great moral reserve. If the masses had made enough of an uproar over this spectacle that we presented, then it would have served to make the point that they would not tolerate such behavior.

"I am greatly disillusioned with the focus that the people of the kingdom have towards being silent over what the royal family does and does not do. I want them to take a greater part in making their wishes known to the House of Commons, Parliament, and the royal family directly. It serves no one well that there is a great discrepancy between the ideals of the people and the ideals of their royalty. I wished that I had my life to do over in this respect. If I had made the same mistakes again that I did before, I would take the lead in making the point that if one does not act like a moral leader for the country, then perhaps they need to be set aside. I am sure that this will not be well received by the majority, but I have no care for that. I think the time has come for the words to be spoken that if one cannot lead with highest integrity then one should step aside and allow another to make the house of royalty an example to be proud of in the world's eyes."

R. "Do you say this because of Charles's behavior? Is this aimed at him?"

**** "I am not directly making this statement at him, for I too have fallen short of the mark. It is no great secret that all who are in line for the throne have fallen short of the mark, except those who are as yet too young to know the pain and responsibility of the throne. I am making this point as an ideal to aim for, and I know that there are many who will interpret this as a personal vendetta against Charles, so I have taken no offense at your question. It is rather a matter of stating how things should be rather than how they have been within the royal family. I do not wish to include the queen in this for I am of great conviction that she has always been of the highest integrity upon this matter. She has known much heartache over the subject of moral breakdown within the royal family, and yet she persists in trying to make them live by a higher standard. I have no qualms with her over this matter and wish to state that I am regrettably very sorry for my own actions that have caused her grief.

"I am simply making the statement that one should be a role model if one is to be upon the throne, and just because the past has given forth examples of those who were in varying degrees of degradation, the future can be changed. I am, if anything, not making this statement for the ones of the past, but for those of the future. I need not remind Charles of this for he has already missed the mark, but I feel it a good thing to make this point to my son and the future king. His is the future of the country, and this is intended to be a message not only to the people, but also to their future leader."

Yes, it would seem that Diana now has no problem speaking out what she thinks. I think that perhaps there would be those who would look at her words about morals and think to themselves, "Sure, she can say that now! She isn't here to take the heat from her own actions." I wonder, though, if this is not an example of hindsight being twenty-twenty, and a sincere effort to make the future better than what she herself was able to do with the past. I feel it is that, as well as an attempt to cover this topic with her son. She would know well that he is being raised to follow his father's footsteps to the throne, but she fervently hopes he follows neither one of their footsteps in his personal life. She must feel, as her sons reach an age of sexual maturity, that she wishes she would be able to guide them through this time with the wisdom she gleaned from her own life. How many of us as parents have turned around and taught our children things that we had to learn the hard way? Would it be any so less for her? How many of us would cringe if we knew our children were even thinking of doing some of the things we did when we were young? Therefore, I feel this to be a sincere effort on her part to have the future learn from the past.

The synchronistic timing of rewriting her words, "Making the point that if one does not act like a moral leader for the country, then perhaps they need to be set aside" did not escape me, in light of the current political situation here in America due to the Clinton scandal. We, here in this country, are strangely facing a parallel dilemma now as we struggle with the decision on how to respond to moral leadership in our ranks. Reading this again for inclusion in this book was somewhat eerie. Perhaps her words about this matter are not only a lesson for people of "the kingdom" and her son, but for the world.

**** "Let us now continue with conviction number two. There is a stance within the kingdom that to work and make money one must be given the will to do so. This is another of those touchy subjects that I could not address while there, so bear with me as I make my point now. It is often held by the powers that make the country operate that if you give too much to the poor then they will simply choose to not work. I am of understanding the theory, but not the purpose that it serves to make this decision for everyone based upon the actions of the few. I want to point out that there are many who would do well with more help from the royal coffers and the government if they were given the opportunity. The ones who would abuse the system would be gleaned out with proper monitoring controls, but for the mass majority it would be a decidedly needed helping hand to bring about the means to further their economic status.

"I am ever increasingly convinced that the difference between those who are poverty-stricken and the ones who are of greatest wealth is the advent of some fortunate breaks at an appropriate time. If the family who needs a financial break were given one for a short time, then their status could be elevated and the whole country would prosper. There are many that could contribute greatly to the whole if they could get beyond the need to work long hours to ensure survival. The help that could be given to them could be in the form of grants and low interest loans to those who are able to contribute something of great need to others, if they could but make the leap from lowest level poverty to the comfort of knowing that there would be enough food if they pursued their greatest gifts.

"Many men need to feel the accomplishment and approval of being of worth, and this is the majority of the ones that I speak for. There shall always be the ones who have no drive or will to succeed, but they shall not be given help beyond what they can produce for the benefit of the whole. There could even be given to some a further wage for public service towards the whole. Things needed such as street cleaning, building restoration, tour guiding, neighborhood patrolling, and a vast number of other services. I have considered this as a function of the foundation and will discuss this further at another session. Our world needs to elevate the world of form into the future of making all work for the whole rather than just for them, and there will be great benefit to all if this can be accomplished. I will now move to my third conviction.

"The third conviction that I hold as being the greatest thing that will make the world function at a higher level of being is the need to make room for their personal search for their spiritual identity. I was not aware of the gifts that I was imbued with from my spiritual source until I came here, but it is possible to make this awareness while there. I am making this my third priority only because there needs to be a focus on the physical world first, then a meaningful search for the purpose and gifts that are given from your own soul for the completion of a very satisfactory life. I am asking that all who are aware of the talents that they have which go beyond their physical knowledge help those who are still seeking to make their own discoveries. I am calling on those such as yourself to help others become aware that all possess gifts that are of the spiritual nature and can implement them into their lives at a benefit for all.

"I was going to suggest this as a function of the foundation, but this is something that must be done with the greatest care by all without outside political influence. It would not be wise to make the foundation a format for this research for it will, of necessity, be given over to many rules and restrictions that are not conducive to the freedom needed to make the proper search for spiritual identity. It can, however, help with the management of the physical life so that persons may have some freedom of time to pursue their spiritual search. The search for their spiritual self will in turn also help with their physical life, and then the gift can be given back to those who still need the help.

"The junction of the foundation and the search for spiritual awareness will not be obvious, of course, but there will indeed be one with the freedom that some will experience through the helping hand from those that they cannot see through the foundation. It is as if you could compare the foundation to the formula that goes into a prayer. There is a request that is given, and if there is great need, then there is a helping of many through the aegis of the foundation so that the request is granted without ever knowing the true source of the help. It is as if there were a spiritual connection given to the powers that hold the ability to help those who have the need, and yet there is never a physical meeting of the two.

The resulting gift of freedom may allow someone to see and feel the power of giving and the effect that it can have upon another's life. This in turn shall foster the feeling of giving to another to help them. I am aware that this sounds very utopian, but I have great faith that this formula will in time help others to raise their sights a little higher, their goals a little farther away, and their need to be of service a little closer. There can indeed be a reformation to the benefit of the whole if there is a focus of finding their spiritual gifts and the time to do so. I am now finished with my soliloquy and will entertain your questions.

R. "Thank you for sharing your convictions. I am well impressed with these, at first consideration, and I think along these same lines myself sometimes. I assume this is to be our last session, so is there anything else that you have remembered about the accident that you want to add?"

**** "I am not going to recount my version of the story as it was given to you, but I do wish to add another facet. There was a great will to make me live by the medical staff and I thank them for this, but I wish them to know that if they had done any more or any less, the end result was to be the same. It was not intended by my soul to continue on in that world, but to come here for the purpose that we have been discussing. There was a great feeling of loss for them, and I wish to tell them that I am well pleased with their performance and their feelings of grief for my family and myself. I am now content with this issue and will answer another question."

R. "Are there any further forms of proof that you are who you say you are that you wish to offer? Any changes to the ones you have given?"

**** "I am well aware that there can never be enough proof for all people, but I am content with what I have given you thus far. It is an attempt to make you feel that I am who I have said that I am, and if you require more I shall think of something else to try and help you. Is there some area that you feel doubt? I can only say that since we have never met within that world, and you are not well versed with my life there, then I have very little to give you that would be conclusive proof until you cross-reference with those who knew me and my life."

R. "Point well taken. What about the discrepancy of going to the airport and the speculation that you and Dodi were going back to his apartment? Do you have any further comments?"

**** "I do not well remember where we were going that evening, I can only remember wanting to wear the ring to the airport. Perhaps I intended to wear it all evening and also to the airport the following day. I have no further comments to this except that it does not matter where we were going—we never got there."

R. "Another point for you! I guess that is true. I can think of no further questions right now, so I will close these sessions by saying thank you for them. I am honored to have been entrusted with what is enclosed in these, and I will protect them with my highest ability. If you have need of me, let me know, as I feel that you did this morning through my dreams. I will periodically check in with my old friend. We have established a bond and I feel honored for that as well. May you have good fortune with your plans and the project as a whole. I am here at your service when you need me. This project is of worthy value and I feel great pride at having the role that you have assigned me. Until we meet again, I will think of you fondly."

**** "I am well aware of your feelings, but I must add that I am concerned that you feel so highly honored. It is not that you are serving someone who is above you, but rather that you are serving those who need the help of those who know of the spirit world and its bounty. I am indeed in your debt for the time that you have given me and will always think of you with great affection also. There is a very powerful miracle here for us to have made the connection that we have, and I feel that to have a friend of your caliber in any world is a form of miracle. We are both blessed by your gift and there will be many who will make use of your gift. I can only hope that you shall find the time to check in with me once our project is at completion. There will be many who seek to use you but remember that one must always live their lives for themselves, and not solely for the masses if they are to feel enriched. I have made that mistake and wish not to see you follow in my footsteps. It is always a great thing to help others but remember that you also have those of your world who need you to be their mother, their friend, their wife. I am going to close by saying that if there is ever any way that we may meet when you get here, I shall be of great satisfaction in knowing that I will have a true friend in this world also. Make your life happy and do what you can for the masses but allow no one to rule your life except yourself.

There is never any wrong for being who you are, and always remember that it was I who told you that. Goodbye and good day until we have the occasion to sit and chat."

Her three convictions listed here in these pages are just that, her convictions. She makes the statement that they sound utopian, and perhaps they do. However, it seems that it has always been humankind's right and inborn nature to dream, desire, strive towards, and attain that which begins only in their thoughts. It is through the conception of thoughts that our world is reshaped and changed continually. It is often true that the higher the ideals, the more profound the changes. It is exactly because they are utopian in nature that they have the inherent potential to elevate the world once again. Beginning where humankind was at any given moment, and searching for utopia, is perhaps how we have arrived here. Beginning where we are now, and still seeking the state of utopia, may be what finds us there one day.

CHAPTER 18

Progress Report, Bitterness of
Betrayal, Foul Weather

It was not until February of 1998 that I spoke to Diana again. The first contact at this time occurred on the eleventh of that month and was surprisingly as clear as it had been prior to the break of such duration in our communication. I was not sure if, after this length of time, there would be a difference in the ease or quality of reception of her words to me. I truly had no idea and was gladdened to see that time did not seem to diminish the connection, or our rapport. She offered me an update to the status of her work with another, which was a curiosity that had been floating through my mind in the preceding months.

R." I want to speak to my friend Diana. Can this be made available to me at this time?"

****. "I am here and so very glad that you have given me the opportunity to converse with you again. I have been very busy with the will of another to make my words seem like his imagination sometimes that I have not been of interest to work with you. This is only because I have had so little else to say upon the matters that we have discussed. I was wondering if you have given it any thought to going with this information as a book and not working with our original plan? I am, myself, disposed to considering this more of an option than earlier for I have been quite busily trying to get another to receive my words with the clarity that you have always received them. I am still working with this person and we are making good progress, but it is indeed slow going as a matter of contrast to our correspondence. I was wondering if you would reconsider this as an option, and if so, would you like to use this as a way to make yourself famous? I would be the first to make you aware that being famous does indeed have its setbacks, but I am sure that you already know this."

R." Are you saying that you do not think the original plan of using three of us to be effective?"

****. "I am saying that it has taken me longer to make the others aware of my words and messages to them, but we shall persevere with this original plan. I was wondering though if you would consider also doing a book for me from this information and allow me a further chance to get this message out to the kingdoms. I want you to know that if you were to do this that there may be great financial rewards, but that there will also be a form of tyranny within this due to the reaction of the majority of the people. I would remind you that if you are within the public eye that you are also open for scrutiny by the media and the powers who would have you be less than what you are. I am sure that you know that I am able to use another for this work, but my first and most desirable choice would be yourself. If you would but consider this as an option, this is all that I could ask from you. If you should decide that you are not wanting to do this for me, I would understand that it is no reflection of our friendship, but a decision based on your concern for your own life. I remember well that it is important to live your life for yourself and this is as it should be. Make no mistake, I am willing to work with another, but would much prefer to work with you. Give this some thought and some time, and we shall meet again to analyze what you have decided."

R." Can you tell me anything about what is going on with the search for the other car? I do not hear any more about this as a rule, and I was wondering what you knew."

****. "I am greatly dismayed that they have not been able to make the connection of the other car to us, but the truth is there. I am now convinced that if they work at getting the former man who was with us that night that he would remember the other car. I was well aware of this car and I know he was also. His memory has been blocked for some time now, but I feel that if he were stimulated to relive the events that he would recall the car. I understand that they have given up on finding the car due to some misinformation, and this is of great concern for me. I was with them when they decided this and I tried to affect the mind of the man who made the decision to halt the search, but I have little effect upon those who do not know that I can speak to them."

(Interesting note: As of this editing, 2005, it was apparent that the bodyguard, Trevor Reese-Jones did regain his memory, or at least partial forms of it, for he has written a book that was released a few years ago. Some speculation exists that he remembers more than he discloses. Some controversy exists over his account of things as he states them. The answers to those things lie solely with him, I suppose. However, I am told that there is no mention of another car in his book.)

> R. "Do you still want me to wait for a sign that your other "channel" has spoken to you? Will it still happen as you had planned?"
>
> **** "I am of working with him as we speak and have made great headway. He is not one who can as easily work with this world yet and he is often fighting the words that I send him. We shall continue as we have planned, and I think that you will recognize the words that I have given to him if he makes this known to the world at large. When you have been given his words from me, I will then give you your part of this to bring to fruition. I am going now to work with him even more fully and will be in touch with you again. All is still as we have planned, but not as easily as I might have hoped it would be. I am well aware that you wait patiently, and I am also aware that you are waiting for further instructions. Thank you for this and may you have another gift of joy when you see that it is as I have said it would be. It is a work that I will accomplish…so make the use of your time now to be of help to others. This is my pledge to you. If there is a time when we can be of service to each other, then I shall always be there for you as you have been there for me."

Shortly after this conversation, I had caught a tidbit on the news that seemed to contradict what she had said about her plans to marry Dodi Fayed. Still testing the waters of accuracy, even after all of the time and conversations that had passed, I had a need to address this with her. Thus, on the sixteenth of February 1998, I made contact and explained why I had "called" again so soon and asked her what she had to say concerning this discrepancy.

**** "I am well aware that someone from within my famous circle of friends has decided to achieve some attention, but it is as I should have expected. I was never forthcoming with many of my friends on the greatest of secrets of my life for this was the very thing that I would have feared most. The influence of fame and power are hard to resist and if they had any feelings for me they would have divulged nothing that was ever told to them. Remember well that I was betrayed by one that I trusted when the tapes were given to the media. I never knew exactly who had betrayed me, but there was no way to ascertain that I had anyone to trust. The incident with the tapes taught me well to confide the real truth of my life with no one....I realized too late that to tell anyone anything that mattered was to lend one's self to vulnerability.

"I cannot say that what has been reported was not true, for this is what this person was told. If I had the intent to marry Dodi, I knew better than to tell anyone for this gave them too much power over my life. If they were told the opposite, then this had no power to affect the truth of my reality. There will be many things that will cause you to doubt what you and I have shared but remember that not all of what you will hear bears a resemblance to what was actually within my heart or my intentions. I am one to keep my own counsel, and after having tasted the bitterness of betrayal, I knew that to divulge anything of importance to anyone would be to invite that foulness into my life once again. Remember only what I have told to you and seek out the truth from the source. All others have only the mirror image of me that I wanted them to see."

R. "That is why I asked you. Thank you for your answer to me."

**** "It is a fine thing to want to know the truth but realize that the truth about me and what I thought and felt and experienced can only reside within me. Others had only what I wanted them to see after I awoke from the dream of being the fairy-tale princess who would live happily ever after. I have no reason to feel intimidated with telling you or the others who will work with me the truth for none of what you have, or know, can affect my life as I know it now. This is the realm of truth, and therefore the lies and misrepresentations of that world do not affect me any longer. You are a wise person and I feel you know that what I say is true.

"Why should I divulge something like that to a friend if it were true? Would that not make my life more complicated to set aside time to be with Dodi if I had no intention of being happy? I wanted to find some personal happiness for myself and to do so I had to keep the world from finding out too soon what I had found for myself. There were always those who wanted to undermine me and my effect upon the kingdom. If this is not answer enough to you and your friends as to why I have not disclosed the relationship to Dodi with any accuracy to those who might come forth to repudiate it, then I can say no more. The truth resides in our lives and that is what will always matter to me."

This made sense to me. I do suppose that one who lives in the lens of public scrutiny would develop the armor to insulate themselves from as much intrusion into their private lives, thoughts, and feelings as they possibly could. Not tipping her true intentions on something so personally held to those who did not have a need to know would make good sense, not to mention lessening the chances of the "bitterness of betrayal." Again, I was given a glimpse into a world that I had never encountered and hope to never know. How sad it must be to have to keep the most important, the most depressing, and the most joyous things locked inside without the outlet of sharing them with someone for fear of betrayal. This once again created a compassion within me for how isolated she must have felt on many occasions.

The next occasion that I had to speak to Diana came on March 31, 1998. In the middle of the conversation, another form of potential proof was offered to me. There was no way that I could ascertain the validity of it, since she again says that the ones who know of this are few. It seemed that she offered it to me, not so much to prove to myself that her words were true, but rather as a figurative "ace up the sleeve" should I find the "hand" that I was holding in doing a book project needed a winning edge. I will record for you most of the conversation but some of the actual details I withhold, not knowing if there is validity to this entire issue. It may be a matter of some delicacy if this is indeed an actual event, and therefore will only discuss the details with the ones who I am sure may know of it. It was not offered as proof to the populace as a whole, just to those who may have the knowledge of this occurrence, if it is indeed an actual event.

*** . "I am here with you and would require that you give me an answer about your thoughts upon doing a book for me out of this form of correspondence. I am working at getting our fellow to make the attempt to contact the former hounds of my life and follow through on our formulated plan of action. I am well aware of the effect this is having upon your life having to sit and wonder if I am who I have said that I am. I will follow through upon our agreed idea of making the world feel my presence, and I would beg that you follow through upon yours.

"I am having a difficult time with the forerunner of our program, for he is often thinking that I am a figment of his imagination, and that if I were really who I said that I am, I would have used someone else who had more notoriety than he. I have tried to explain that he is not the only one who has heard my voice, so to speak, but he is vacillating upon the wisdom of going to the press with this material. I am well informed that they have begun to believe that I am working with others, but the proof that they seek is not being given them. I am wondering if that will be a problem. I want so badly for them to work with me, and I have requested that their advisors be given the will to help me in this venture. It will yet be some time for this to become known, and so I ask for your forbearance for another few months."

How well I understood the emotional upheaval that she describes this other as experiencing! I imagine that I had at least a three- to four-month head start on him with regard to having time to integrate the idea that I had Diana "on the line," so to speak. At this point in my journey with her and our communications, I was still facing bouts of questioning and incredulousness over the whole matter. Therefore, I knew intimately how he might be feeling since I had been there in the not so long ago past. I felt some pity for him knowing the mind-bending feeling that it was to work at rationalizing this whole affair and deal with it logically. However, I have to also admit to feeling a wee bit of mirth thinking about whether he was wondering if he was going crazy!

**** "Give this some thought: If they should follow through on their thoughts of making this known only if and when they are sure that others have been spoken to by myself, will you follow through on your end by being the one to take the lead? I am requesting this only as a last resort and still have in mind to make you the follower rather than the forerunner. It is imperative to me that someone steps up to the front and acquires the courage to be the forerunner for this project. I am currently working on the others, and if I am successful, then our conversation shall be null and void of import. If they should lag behind for fear of obvious reasons, can I count upon you to work at putting together a book for our project? It will make a far-reaching impact and they will then be given the proof that they need. Once this has occurred then they too will claim to have the same material, and this will lead the world to know that one source gave many outlets the power of being the fairy-tale princess's voice of reason.

"I am aware of the import that you place upon your own forms of proof, and so I propose to make you aware of something that no other has yet made known to the world. This is a form of proof again that bears little weight with any but those who are knowing about it but holds great weight with the royal family. If they are concerned with the source, then they will find the formula to make you aware of the validity of the statement. I was going to use this in my book and would like now to share it with you. There was a man who approached me about doing a book about the royal family and their preoccupation with the more important aspects of their history."

R." I don't understand how a book on the family's history and preoccupation with it could be so threatening. Can you give me some clarity about why?"

**** "I was told that the man intended to work with me for the sake of having my name attached to his work…The man who wanted to do the book wanted me to disclose this sort of history and the effects that it had upon the royal family from my point of view.

"When one knows what lies in the closet, then one can adequately choose what to put on when the weather turns nasty. When the winds began to grow cold and the rain to fall, I chose just the appropriate garment to protect myself. It is all a matter of being in the right closet when the need arises. This is a form of proof that will mean little to any except the family, but I am offering this to you in case we need a little foul weather protection. If you should have to go public with any of my material, this would give you some protection from the winds of Windsor. If they knew that you were privy to this information they could readily see that I am offering to you the same form of protection that I chose. It is all a matter of being in the right know when the reality demands it.

"If we are to do this project then we need to assume that there may be stormy weather from the castle walls and having a rubber to protect us would not be untoward. Give my thoughts to you today some thought and we shall speak again. I am well aware that you wait patiently for my completion of my foray into the realms of another's mind, and I thank you for this. The arrival of the anniversary of my death approaches, and I have determined that this should be our deadline. If they will not come forward with what they know, then we shall have to take a new directive. We shall speak of this soon enough. Good day to you, and may we have another good chat then."

Again, I can make no claim to the validity of what she said to me during the last half of this conversation. Some of what was said I have withheld; other parts of her statement are exposed. It is included in here for these reasons: It is a large segment of transcript. It seems as if it could be proof, if found valid, that contact had been made, and most importantly, because it seemed important to her to offer this as an attempt of proof for some. The details are not important to this book as a whole, unless verified, and even then they may remain with Diana, those who have the knowledge of what she speaks, and myself. It is not an attempt to frustrate the reader, build suspense, create mystery, or anything else. It is solely my attempt at discretion in the face of not knowing what to do with some of this information. It appears to me that it is far better to err by holding my peace than to err by speaking of something that I have no firsthand knowledge of.

Once again, she had broached the subject of me doing a book. I did not give her an answer that night, or for many months to come. I was in the frame of mind to wait for this other who had been mentioned to put his neck on the chopping block first by going public with the knowledge that he had spoken to her. As the months rolled by, I was being patient, not only because of her request to do so, but also due to cowardice. If someone else would do it, why rush forward and throw myself down on my knees in front of the chopping block? Cowardice is the better part of saving your neck, sometimes.

To avoid the topic of having to reach a decision, or having to discuss this with her again, I adopted the stance of not speaking to her for another four months. I waited and watched the headlines, fervently hoping to see the release of information that someone was claiming to have made a connection to the deceased princess. However, as the time expanded, so did my desire and my impatience to get this matter settled. Curiosity grew stronger than the desire to bury my head in the sand and not speak to her, so in July of 1998 I sat at the computer to chat with the princess who had taken up space in my heart.

2019 Addendum:

The male that she mentions, the one she tells me would take the lead of her work was finally found by me in 2005 after a seven-year span of looking. When I saw his website I knew, just knew, that he has been speaking to Diana for some things dovetailed with what I had been given. So, I wrote to him. I had a great shock though for I discovered not only did Diana speak to him, as she did to me, but also spoke THROUGH him. He is a voice channel and hearing Diana address me via a phone call a bit later after reaching out to this man almost knocked me off my chair.

That man is Andrew Russell Davis and he is the only direct voice channel for Diana. Much of our work with Diana, after joining forces, can be found at DianaSpeaks.info.

CHAPTER 19

Open Forum, New Agenda,
Overall Picture of Creation

long this whole journey of time, there were always odd and interesting things happening that concerned Diana in some way. These consisted of events such as people who had no knowledge of my channeling experience with her telling me some tidbit or another about her. Often they would mention something that had developed or occurred that gave credence to information logged within my computer. It seems what I had missed on the news was handed to me by someone who came into my realm of daily activity.

One strange incident that seemed very synchronistic to me was when a client of mine walked in and handed me a stack of old tabloids from many months previous. She then stated that she would bring me future issues after she had read them. I had never purchased these except for an occasional one once every year or so. They were never my choice of recreational reading, and I do little recreational reading anyway. When the controversy over the tabloids hounding her, even while she lay bleeding, and the subsequent boycott began, I had determined that I also would not buy any more out of respect for her. However, when the woman gave me the bag and I opened it and almost every issue had something to do with Diana, I realized that this just might be more than a coincidence. So I read them and again discovered things that made sense with what I had been told. Thus, when I had the next conversation with Diana I approached this subject with her.

R. "Hello, Diana. I have thought of you often and have been given copies of the tabloids to read. I find it interesting that I have previously purchased very few of these in my life, and when I decided that I would not buy them again because of you, someone begins giving them to me. I had to look at this as a sign or omen and have read what I could about you in them. It seems that your friend Dodi's father has raised some interesting questions about the circumstances of your death. I think he knows, or feels, as you have said, that someone or something formed an effort to take you out of the picture. What do you have to say to me today?"

**** "I am well aware of the gifts that you have been given and this is of and in itself the reason that you have been given them. I am aware that you do not follow the world's preoccupation with the seamier sides of people and do not find it pleasurable to read the tabloids as a practice of regularity. I was wanting you to find the keys that I have given you within these and so I have had some help in getting them delivered to you. I have been working with our fellow friend in an effort of getting him to make an effort to come forward with what he has received, but he is of finding it within himself to fear the consequences. I would therefore like to ask that you give it over to your consideration to find within you the courage to make this form of communication that we have established into an open forum. This is an attempt to make this known to the ones who have worked with me and are yet unwilling to come forward to substantiate the words that I have given them."

R. "What do you mean by 'an open forum'?"

**** "I am referring to making this communication public knowledge. This can be done in forms of writing letters to the future heralders of my wishes, to the press corps of these tabloids, to the ones who are of being able to find my words authentic, and to the ones who were my former family. It can also be done through the book that I have asked you to formulate, or through releasing this to my father's friend whom I have given my utmost trust. I would prefer that you work with my words as being able to stand for themselves, and to not fear the reprisals that are only of being within your mind. I am given reassurances that our work together would bring you no harm, and I have pledged myself to this. I would find it of utmost importance to find you no worse for the helping of me and my cause.

"I have another agenda now that I have been given some time to think and to find the truth of my existence. I was able to find that my open-minded way of seeing the world was not the cause of my demise as much as the open-minded ways that they had of being able to see that I needed to make the gifts of my popularity work for the kingdom instead of against the priorities of the established monarchy. I was too self-willed to allow them to get the best of me and not let them feel my presence. I wanted them to see that I had left the castle, but not the kingdom. I was wanting them to see that if they had the best of the people in their hearts that we could do much to eradicate the fear of being alone and poor, wretched and abused. I wanted to open the minds of the kingdom that not all who would put upon their shoulders the mantle of royalty would forget the ones who were the subjects of their rule.

"I was wrong to assume that I could change an ongoing aristocracy without having to pay for the insult upon the powers that ruled. I have no fear for you over these issues for there is now a time to be had that can and will erase the fears of those things that I fought so hard against. Your betrayal will not be forthcoming from any man who would stand against me, but from the realm of your own limitations. I have given this considerable forethought and have reached the conclusion that our work will find the needed reception within the hearts of those who seek to change the forms of power that need to be changed.

"I was once set upon vengeance for what I had seen as a wrong. I am now of the wisdom and heart to make the things I had seen as right become the focal point for our work. I want now to thank the world that I had inhabited for allowing me to become the fairy-tale princess and giving me the fortitude to find inside myself the need to further the work of what was right over that which was of always being. Given this as a basis of focus, we shall exclude the need to seek vengeance over wrongs but work at finding more of the features within the kingdom that are righteous and needed to be added to. Our focus will now not be what should change, but what should continue.

"It is a far greater thing to uplift that which is good than to try and destroy that which is not wanted. I have been given the advice by this world that to work against something only gives it more power, whereas working towards something good will also increase the power and scope of things needed within that world. Our work will continue to support what is needed and focus the harnessed energies of those who are with this vision into a group that finds only the good and chooses to make it the prevalent focus. With this as our focus, there can and will be greater things accomplished.

"It matters not why I was taken from that world, because I was meant to come here to this world to continue my work. I was well established as the fairy-tale princess and had built my foundation of needed strength within the kingdom and the world. I had overcome the ending of my royal journey and had found the peace that I had been seeking. I had accomplished what I had wanted and was finding people receptive to me and to my views. I needed to leave that world as an icon to establish the need within the people to want to continue my causes and to ensure the future of the things that I had started. I am now at peace with the transition of my energy and do not fear for my former works. They will continue and I can add to them from the source of the infinite wisdom that is possessed by those who work from this level of understanding.

"I have been given a glimpse of what may become, and I could ask no more for my kingdom and my sons. I have been graced with an understanding of why they have been given to your world and I find it a future that I could only have been responsible for if I had been precisely who I had been. I am at peace with them being who they chose to be and I would rescind my for-

mer view to you that I had given them life with
no future choice. I have the understanding now
to know that when they were given to me based
on upon their own wisdom of what they wanted
to do and why they had to come to be the sons of
the fairy-tale princess.

"It is far clearer when one thinks, not with
their mind as it is limited within the body, but
with the mind as it exists in the entire overall picture of creation. I have been given the grace to
know that I have been one with what I intended
to do and had accomplished my goals as a soul
who journeyed to the land of the future kings
and the common man to aright the needed
imbalances. It will be as it has been given to me
if we work at finding the needed attributes of the
kingdom and the world and focus away from the
inferior failings of man to understand the process
of being given the greatness within them."

How inspiring that last sentence of hers is! Her eloquence with
some of her statements and ideas upon things has always inspired
me to my own thoughts of a better world. I could only wish to have
this gift of being able to express ideas in such a marvelous way to
inspire that type of feeling in someone. This attribute of using words
so simply, and yet so powerfully is one of the ways that I knew that I
had contacted her. I had to admit to myself that in my best creative
endeavors, I would never be able to put things in that form of wonderful rhetoric. As I said much earlier in this book, I have chosen
predominantly to use her own words. How could I match the power
of some of her statements, or relay the real emotions that are inherent
within her words of disillusionment, anger, anguish, and motherly
concerns? I knew better than to even try.

Did you notice, as I did, her newer views and the sense of peace
that came through in this conversation? It would seem that her time
there in that world had done much in helping find a sense of inner

peace and she had been given the knowledge that she needed for this to be so. This is not an uncommon idea, either to religion, or to those of us in the world that can and does speak to the ones who have passed on and inhabit the world of spirit. I have often seen the results from when loved ones here realize that they have spoken to their deceased loved ones, and yet are amazed and relieved to hear the positive change in their loved one's attitude.

Much of our unrest in this world comes from the unrest within someone's inner self as they react or behave in ways that are induced through unhappiness or lack of self-worth. To hear that she had found peace with what had at first seemed so pressing on her about her son's lives was a warm feeling for me. It had been this that had first made me feel deeply for her, and I was able to rejoice with her as she basked in her newfound knowledge and peace. The change in her from the beginning of our communication and this writing does tend to reinforce the concept that heaven, or the world of spirit, is a place of healing and infinite knowledge, doesn't it? Perhaps through her words we have all been given a glimpse of what it is like to not see through the "glass darkly."

CHAPTER 20

Robes of Royalty, Upon the Weaver's Loom

I t was this transcript dated August 20, 1998, that launched me into the writing of this book. Almost an entire year had passed since having first met Diana in the vestibule of thought that rests between this world that we know as real and the world that is real in a way that we have no recollection of while here. I had often stepped into this vestibule, but the shock of having the world's most famous woman standing there to greet me was an immense one. I suppose that I had thought that someone like her would be swept off into the castles and palaces in the sky! To find that she was loitering in the vestibule waiting for someone to speak with and to find kinship with was a concept that would never have occurred to me. I have often humorously likened it to the feeling of going to the grocery store with the ugliest of clothing on, no makeup, hair that had seen better days, and finding yourself face-to-face with an incredibly handsome movie star who finds you charming and attractive. This stuff just doesn't happen to me in real life. Not to this peon from the suburbs!

The fact that it took me almost a full year and more than fifty hours of conversation with her to rest secure in the knowledge that she had indeed found it within herself to speak to me tells the story of how surprised that I was. Like the fantasy of meeting the gorgeous movie star at the grocery store, it was an event that gave rise to major internal questioning, feelings of euphoria, self-doubt, wonder, and the knowledge that it would never be forgotten. However, by the time that this latest transcript was written, I had gained the mental and emotional equilibrium to say, "Hey, why not me? It was just a matter of being in the right place at the right time with someone who was willing to see me for who I could be." Thus, I had made the decision to follow her lead and see what else our journey together would unfold. I had decided to do this book and not listen to the fear that had always kept me bound into the comfort zone that I had always inhabited.

R." Diana, I am here to speak to you and want you to tell me what you need to tell me first. I will ask questions later. Consider me an open vessel for your thoughts."

**** "I am so pleased that you can and will allow me this moment within your form of existence to speak to you of our work. There are many things occurring that I have to make clear to you so that we may pursue our intended goal.…If you would be willing to work with our words together as being the epitome of what I have intended to say, then we may now work at making them publicly known. I would request that you give them to the world in the form of a book and mention that I have added the substance while you have provided the filler.

"It is with great joy that I have been made aware of your ability to make this a priority for our work and I shall redeem myself to you for having to wait so long and so patiently. I am now prepared to give you the gift of knowing why I have selected you for this project and I have full faith in your abilities to find this amusing. You were so kind to me with your feelings when I first approached you that I knew then that the world would have the feelings of my words through you. You were able to relate to me with your experience as a mother and as a woman who had suffered many great burdens of her own. I have chosen you for your mix of faith and loyalty to your beliefs. I have chosen you for your ability to look at things and yet not become ensconced with only the feeling aspect of what your emotions would have you believe. You are also a very amicable person and should be able to relate well with all who should encounter you for this work.

"I am also proud to say that we have many things in common that are very important for the work of receiving the world as it is and finding a better way for it to be. You are also one who can be trusted with this process for you have not gone public with the details of our relationship and have waited for my wishes to be given to you. You must understand that this is a value that I still find of utmost importance since I had so few within my earthly realm that I felt I could truly trust."

She was correct. After some contemplation upon her words, I did find the humor of why she had found me suitable for this work. Her words about my responding to her emotionally when we first spoke were true. It was the emotional aspects that served as the bait that kept bringing me back.

Her assertion that I had related to her as a woman who had borne many great burdens was one of those hindsight ironic twists that I do find so laughable. Not to bore you with details that are of no consequence now, I will only say that in one short segment of time in my life I had found myself standing in the ashes of all that I knew. Every area of my life—financial, personal, being someone's child, mental, and spiritual—were torn asunder and deposited at my feet for me to trip over. It had been my children and their dependency upon me that had been the glue that had held this shattered soul together. The humor from her words came when I realized that my emotional trip to hell, purgatory, and limbo had perhaps been the red carpet rolled out for a reception with a royal princess. It had always felt more to me like having been in the Land of Oz and finding the yellow brick road had ended in a garbage dump and the munchkins were credit collectors!

Her kind words about faith and loyalty to my beliefs struck me as a nice way of telling me that my stubbornness about changing my mind once it was made up was a good trait in her eyes. But most of all, her words about my having been trustworthy with her words to me boiled down to being the funniest of all. What she was referring to as trustworthiness had at the onset been cowardice! Not to say that I had not attempted towards the trust that she was referring to, but much of my silence and lack of going public had initially been due to the less than honorable trait of fear. I knew by her suggestion that if I were to find the humor in her words that I had to look deeper than her words for the irony that she had hidden in there. We had established that we both liked irony, and so when I unraveled her words, I saw the humor.

It also strikes me that she was, and is, capable of seeing people for their best traits through the layers of grime surrounding them from their outer circumstances and inner failings. This is a trait that is shared by all great humanitarians. This is the attribute that made her able to care so deeply for those who had lost sight of their own light, their own self-worth. By lending her vision of their beauty and worth to the world, and her own light, she was able to make them and others see a glimpse of the hidden gleam of the higher reflection in the eyes of God.

> **** "I am able to say with great pride that your friends are to be commended for their ability to help you with correcting your viewpoint that you are an accomplished forerunner for the world of spirit. I have taken delight in your achievements of working with this world for others besides myself. I have indeed been aware

of your other projects and have been given this privilege by your advisors. I have learned to work well with your advisors and have their full cooperation on our project. If they were to be of any objection, then I would have not been so forward with my form of communication to you. I have no need to think that if I want something that I can make it happen simply because I was the former fairy-tale princess. I had learned that lesson while I was there. The robes of royalty were not so much symbols of freedom and superiority to me as they were symbols of suffocation and oppression. There were good things that came from my life there, but the robes were only the stepping-stones for me after I had learned not to trip myself with them.

"I wanted to tell you that much will be required from you for the forming of this future foray into finding our voices heard. It will require that you become dedicated to forming the book, finding the courage to formulate your own ideas and thoughts about my form of existence, and the need to feel secure with what you know to be the truth with your heart. I have given you the forms of repression that I had to live under; I want you now to find within yourself the forms of repression that you live under. It is easy for me to say that we have much in common, but it is now up to you to find the reasons that I have made this claim. I want this to be a reformation within you as well as the world. Let not the world see me as having been one who wanted to work only for the United Kingdom, but for all who had need. If you can follow my lead we shall have a reformation for all who have need, including ourselves. As we work for the uplifting of the downtrodden, we shall be uplifted. It was one of the greatest lessons that I learned there in your world and I mean to continue with this for myself and those who are willing to learn it with their hearts and not just with their minds.

"May we have success with this project for the future will be aided in ways that have yet to unfold, but I have had the grace to find these truths within the fabric of our formed intellect as a species. This is a formal way of saying that our future is not preordained, but rather upon the weaver's loom. If you know how to weave a beautiful pattern, you shall have a beautiful frock. If we have a beautiful vision of what we want to see at the end of our looms, we shall have a beautiful frock large enough to fit the entire world. I am ready now for your questions."

R. "You do this to me every time. You leave me totally blown away at your words and ability to make them mean so much. I don't really know if you were this eloquent here when you spoke, because I have only heard small portions of a few of your speeches, but if not, can I sign up for the speech-making classes you are taking over there? They must be awesome! So, what format do you want this book to take?"

**** "I would prefer that you use it as a way to follow my words within their general meanings. I do not require that you quote me verbatim, but if that is your preferred method then I shall have no objection. I want you also to use some of your experience with working with this realm as a showcase on how we are able to communicate so well and follow through on getting the readers to understand the essence of what our world is forming for your world. I have great faith in your ability to make this book entertaining as well and remember that I have a great fondness for humor.

"If there are references to the royal family to be made, remember that I have been one of them and do not wish to find myself portrayed as a family basher. I have great respect for them as people, but do not sanction the way that put honor and duty before the finer and higher things of life. Remember well also that I have two sons within that fold and do not wish our words to reflect poorly upon them. I will direct you through these foul waters, but I must insist that you complete most of the book on your own. You have the skills, the information from me, the advice of this world, and the need to make this our voice for the ones who speak but do not get heard. I am ever willing to help you with this project, but I will not write this for you."

Well now, it would seem that we have yet another irony! She had no objection to me using her words verbatim, which I have done for previously stated reasons. In the course of using her words verbatim, she has indeed written this book for me! I did not realize this irony until I reached this segment of the book, and in retyping these words of hers I had the dawning that this last sentence was a humorous one full of the irony that we both love.

**** "The guidelines are as follows: Use the essence of my words with great care, use the words themselves if need be. Do not paint me as a family basher for that would be far from my truest nature. If I had wanted that job done, I could have done it myself with a full arsenal of ammunition. Work with this as a fulfillment for my work while there and follow the letter of the law as to how I have always wanted to find the ways to help those in need. Do not make this a somber and boring work. Use your gift for words and humor to help enliven our principles. There is more gain in a teaspoon of humor than a bucket of boredom. Finally, use this as a focal point for our joint endeavor to express to the world the need within all of us to help those who are of being needy so that we may find no need within ourselves. Ours is the cause that can and will affect the entire world if we can but find the strength and courage to lay the first brick of compassion within the new wall for humanity."

R. "Thank you again for your words. They inspire me to greater thoughts of myself and I believe that our work together may do this for others as well. I must go now and will do what I can for this and will speak to you soon."

**** "I am honored as well to have you with me for this project. Your form of following my words with such ease is indeed a rare commodity and I have done well to have been given you as a form of secretary. I have many things to be thankful for in my state of being, and you are one of the finest, most feeling people I have met. I am glad that even in my death I have been given the gift of knowing one who would not betray me. I have great compassion for those who do not have this honor, and I make this statement from having had an experience where one does not always know where one's enemies are camped.

"I request that you keep this project secret no longer but follow through on your own caution and wisdom as to how this should be handled. If I shall have any doubts about your ability, it would be your need within you to have others find you accurate and reliable. It will be a matter shortly of you finding within yourself the wisdom to know that what you have is correct, and no matter who shall detract from your work, it will not form a feeling of insecurity within you. I have many times been placed there by others and would have you avoid this if you can find the courage to do so. Good biddings to you and I shall find our other friends as I have need of them."

CHAPTER 21

The Peon's Ponderings

We have now come to the end of the main body of transcripts that I received prior to beginning this book. I have spoken to her twice since the beginning of this book for clarification on how to proceed, advice as to whether to include a certain comment or two, and whether there happened to be anything else that she would wish to include other than what I already had. There are two comments from those conversations that I will include here, and this shall be the conclusion of what I have from her to this date.

Her first comment concerns my role as her spokesperson. I had wondered what capacity my role might take once the book was done, and she gave me the answer to this: "I will say here at this juncture that I do not intend to hold forth with interviews through the means of using you as a spokesperson, so have no fear over that issue. I will, however, ask to speak to key members of the founding of my work, and the ones who I feel a need to speak to. It will incorporate those of my family, and I have given you the words before to say to them." This comment from her comes on the heels of other comments about preparing my family and myself for possible media attention once the book was done, and I must say here that her comment about not having to do interviews was a relief. Thankfully, at least as far as her words at that time, this will not be a request that she will make of me.

The second comment was in answer to questions about whether she wanted to add anything else to the book and the material that I already had. "I would indeed be joyous to write an addition for our work of the book. I shall do so when we are almost complete with this drudgery of having to work with the formatting of this fine work. I am well pleased and so shall you be when you see the reaction of those who truly knew me. Thank you again for your friendship and loyalty. I have been well rewarded with you as a friend."

As of this writing, I have not yet worked with her for the receiving of that final addition, and I hope to make those words the final chapter. So, I sit here, even now, in suspense of what she has decided to be the final words to all of us through this book. The suspense is bittersweet in nature, since it is killing me to know what she will say, but I had determined to finish my part of the book, and then bring through this information as a closing statement. It seemed only fitting that her words be the last in a work that she started, she formulated, and she hopes will help others. Since she started this book project, she will close it. That seemed most appropriate to me.

During the journey of recording her words, and even in writing this book, I have had many questions come to mind that I have no concrete answers for, but I have come to some sense of the reason that the questions were there. The questions that this experience raised within me, and the resulting search for answers, were meant to ever widen my perspectives of the world of spiritual communication, and the need for all worlds (physical and spiritual) to work towards the healing of all. It has also made me work at delving into what another person might feel about this material and how to make this odd gift of mine seem almost normal to those who have not had the opportunity to realize that this form of communication does indeed exist, and is not something to fear. Not to be taken lightly is the search for faith enough in myself, and the messages from her, to write this book. Faith enough to stand firm even if there should be derision and adversity with coming forward with this message that I had come to believe was truly from Diana, the "fairy-tale princess."

Had she approached someone else, would they have been so hesitant to believe in the phenomena if they had such a background in working with those of the spirit world as I had? It would not be hard to imagine that someone who had never before found themselves listening to the words of someone deceased finding it far too incredible to handle. I had been there once, so I well know that feeling. But considering my background of relaying information from that realm, why was I so doubtful and frightened on an intellectual level to accept that it was really her, yet so willing to let my heart lead with what it believed? I have the feeling that this is exactly what I was to find. I was meant to find that when dealing with that which is spiritual one cannot impose the standards of what is normal in the physical world when judging that which comes from the spiritual side of man, life, or God. It might be from an emotional level that spiritual truths may best be discerned. Therefore, how much of the spiritual realm do we overlook because it does not fit in with our intellectual reasoning or the scientific models of what is supposed to be? No concrete answer for that one either!

I often wonder about those Diana had mentioned as having made contact with in conjunction with this work, and who, so I am told, have had enough doubts that they chose not to come forward. I do not wonder that they had enough discretion not to do so. That is an easy answer to me since I had been there in that decision-making arena myself. I wonder instead if they will now come forward and give me backup and reveal other words that she has issued to them. I have been told that they will do so, but I wonder if they have found their faith, their will to challenge the commonly held belief systems, and their hidden reasons why this experience was given to them above others who also speak to the world of the spiritual. I wonder if we will find that we have been called to do this work because of our differences or because of the ways that we are the same. The answer to these musings lies in my future, but then again, so does the rest of my life! I look forward to these answers, yet another gift to be unwrapped from this entire episode.

I often wonder if her words will affect the changes that she so fervently hopes that they will. I wonder if, as she has intimated, these changes are also backed by even higher sources than she. I wonder if the reason she came to our attention, became the admired woman that she was, and the humanitarian we knew, was to make precisely that impact so that her work after her death would carry more weight. She seems to say that this is so. I feel quite certain that the answers lay in how the world responds to these words that have been released to us. Words alone have power, but the actions that words stimulate have even a greater power to change physical world outcomes.

As she so eloquently said, our futures are upon the weaver's loom, and how we weave her words into a tapestry of actions for those who need help will show us how wonderful a frock that we can create to clothe the world. Her words about creating our own world were very basic in nature. If we want the world to change and become what we envision, we have to work at not only dreaming of the pattern, we must toil to find the yarns of compassion, giving, tolerance, and love within us to add to the tapestry that is being woven for our futures. As we all weave our own patterns and they are incorporated into the final outcome, then all can look at this work with pride, not solely for the piece that we have woven, but for the fact that we cocreated such a wonderful gift to the world for its enjoyment. Her words that all should give to those who lack so that we would not find lack within ourselves, and that when we uplift others we too may be uplifted, are words that have power but only if they are transformed into action.

I wonder what impact this book will have towards my life. I can imagine many futures from the release of such material, if indeed I find a publisher who will have faith that this is to be given to the market. Some imaginings cause me fear and the return to thoughts of still hiding what I have sat on for this past year and a half. Some are infinitely more pleasant, and I pray that this would be the outcome.

Taking her lead with the admonishment to create my own frock, I have determined to not let the thoughts of others enter the pattern that I have dreamed of with this work. Therefore, it is not what others shall do or say, but rather what I take from this experience. I will focus upon the gifts of generosity that she has inspired with her words and her example. I will dream of the reformation that she has spoken of and will find my own yarns to add to this dreamed-of world. I will try and live up to the vision that she must have had of me when she approached me and asked me to work with her for this project. I will find the ways to make my gifts from her of respect, self-confidence, faith, and a need to work for others take form in my life and those around me. I will continue to take her lead with what we can do, and if it is what I want for my life, we shall work together in the future for extensions to this work that we have barely begun. It is up to me what my life will be like with the release of this book, despite the praises or the rejections that this work will sponsor. Having "known" her, and the feelings that she has given me through her words and ideas, makes me wonder why I have not before tried to live up to my potential for helping others and working to make a better garment for the world to wear.

Wondering still why she spoke to me, when I know good and well that there are many, many others who may have greater skills than I with working with the world of spirit, has brought me to an interesting revelation. Whereas in the early days of working with her I felt so inadequate and like such a peon in the world, I have now come to an understanding of why her choosing someone like me may have in fact been a good thing.

Her reaching out to one such as I, who is an unknown and typically average person, can be seen as a message from her that giving and working for a better world should be done by others than those with fame or vast riches. It is a sign that a grassroots movement from those who are the middle section of humanity may create a critical mass situation that will spread "upward" and "downward" to balance the scales of need and fulfillment. She is speaking in analogy that one is never too far down or too insignificant to make a difference in the world.

As a matter of fact, I have come to realize that Diana recognizes no class distinctions when evaluating a person's true worth as a human being. In this arena anyone can prove themselves as worthy as any king, noble person, billionaire, entertainment star, or princess. It is not how much you give but how much of what you have that you give that matters. It is the giving from the well of compassion that makes one magnanimous, and monetary value is of least importance if you have very little to give from. Diana's friend, Mother Teresa, demonstrated that remarkably well.

I wonder how much religious debate this work will cause. I understand that many religions do not have a basis for belief in speaking to "average" persons who are residing in the realm of spirit, only perhaps in communicating with angels and those higher in status than that. They also do not believe that the "average" person of this world can possess such powers. However, in having spoken to many people who profess one religion or another, I have come to realize that many people have a belief that they have at some time or another felt the presence of one of these "average" individuals, if not a belief that contact was made between themselves. If many people believe this, I wonder why religious doctrine and leaders do not recognize the fact that their "sheep" are seeing something different than the commonly held ideas of spiritual communication.

I know that many have told me that they have not spoken to their religious leaders of such events out of fear. They have admitted to not speaking even to those closest to them for the same reasons. I think that they spoke to me simply because I had asked and was willing to draw them out nonjudgmentally. Since I have the experience to know of these things, then I have no reason to judge. I wonder when the religious leaders will ask their flocks, nonjudgmentally, about their experiences of a spiritual nature and listen to the thoughts of those who do constitute the churches. When will more people in the churches work for their own spiritual understandings rather than have another decide for them what is possible and what is not possible within the realm of the spiritual?

I have even encountered one Catholic father who has had many incredible experiences, but they are yet not recognized by the institution that he represents. Is there a parallel between the robes of religiosity and the robes of royalty that Diana spoke of? Does the fact that any particular religion does not accept such things mean that such things do not exist? I wonder if this work Diana has started is also a way to open that form of debate.

I have wondered if the words that I have recorded in faith as being those of Diana will be proven to be valid communication. Perhaps there is no sure way to establish this. I do know that I was told several things, such as the fact that the bodyguard would awaken from the coma and about a second car, well in advance. It was given to me to know from her of a second car when reports here in the United States had not yet covered that as being a facet of the accident. There were little things that she said to me that were later found in some coverage of her life, or in the words of others who knew her, that gave me the faith to feel that her words to me were real. These things were given to me in advance so that I would know that I had not created the story. They were the signposts that helped me to establish my own personal level of proof in the origin of these words being outside of me. There may never be proof enough for the world, but proof is only necessary for those who really knew her. These are the forms of proof that I wish for and can only wonder if they will be fulfilled.

I run now only on faith that it shall be so. I wonder if this has not happened to make me strengthen my faith, not only in the existence of Diana's being and the being of others after physical death, but in all things that are not based in the physical world. Faith has a way of atrophying if it is not exercised. This has been a major workout to tighten my faith in my abilities, the celestial helpers I have come to know, ideologies not commonly held in the religious sector, and the fact that I and all others can weave our ideas of a better world into something befitting our status as the highest of God's earthly creations. I wonder how this work might help others exercise their faith in similar ways, and the ways that are needed for them.

I wonder if my faith will remain strong in myself if there is no forthcoming proof of the validity of her words. That may well be the truest test of my faith. However, working out the "muscles" of faith simply for a short time yields only short-term results. If it should happen that no one can prove the validity of her words to themselves, or to others, it will be just another exercise for me to work on my own faith in what I believe to be true, and that all things happen for a reason. Actually, faith is exactly that, having belief in things not readily proven, that makes no logical sense, or that you have no control over. As a very eloquent speaker once said, "Now faith is the substance of things hoped for, the evidence of things not seen.... Through faith we understand that the worlds *(note: This is plural!)*

were framed by the word of God, so that things which are seen were not made of things which do appear" (Hebrews 11:1, 3; KJV).

I aspire to this speaker's level of faith. I work diligently on faith knowing that many have had struggles with things not beheld or witnessed before. This speaker himself had to struggle with the parallel phenomena of someone speaking to him from beyond an earthly grave, though such things were not seen as possible. He remained firm and unshakable. I wonder where many of us would have been if his faith had faltered or the faith of men like Edison, Bell, Einstein, Gates, to name a few. My faith remains firm at this point in what I have experienced and what I have gained from this adventure of having spoken to Diana. I have faith that it will do so for the future.

Lastly, I would not be honest if I said that I would not wonder what each and every one of you would think of the content of this book. I know that many may scoff at the thought of speaking to the spirit world since there is no scientific proof (as of yet) for this phenomenon, and many religions do not recognize it for the average individual. Those who will scoff may have not had an experience either personally or through someone else who was able to bring convincing enough evidence through for them to have given them their own level of proof for belief. They may well be the sorts to dispatch the entire idea of this book before they get beyond the first chapter. I can understand their need for proof, but not their lack of willingness to work at disproving it by exploring as far as they can to fairly decide if it exists or not. It was exactly this attitude of investigation that led me further into the labyrinth of discovery into my own abilities.

Others will read this and wonder if this is fiction or an attempt to claim fame and riches. I also would have similar thoughts had I not been the one sitting in my chair and had not been there firsthand. For those in this "fiction" bracket of readers, I have this response: Let us suppose, for the sake of argument of course, that this was a work of fiction, intentional and deliberate. This would be a fictional work that encompasses the envisioning of a better world, reminders to find the humanitarian in each of us, the view that even the wealthy and the royal bear some form of afflictions in their lives as well as all of us. It highlights some of the joys and sorrows that one may encounter in life. It celebrates motherly love, searching for love that fulfills, helping those who need a hand, and judging by the soul and not by the circumstances. It denounces seeing one's self as superior to another in the eyes of God due to earthly status, interfering with someone trying to do good, and forgetting to be who we truly could be if we looked inside ourselves and outward towards others. For those who think that this is a fictional work of my creation, I am honored. That you have the faith that I could have done such a grand work as this on my own makes me smile. However, badly as I wish that I could take the credit, I cannot. My word may mean nothing to those who do not know me, but I swear that this story is real. I, therefore, can take credit only for the words that I have added, delineated clearly for you by a different form of typeset.

Another response comes to mind for those who would say that I made this up to try and grab fame and rewards of monetary value. My fear has been that I shall find infamy rather than fame with its more pleasant aspects. No one would deny that fame has its rewards, but the honest, sane person would also know that it has some major drawbacks. Many in the public eye would trade that fame for some privacy and normalcy in their lives. Many have done this very thing. I can assure you that I dread the fame almost as much as the infamy if this work is ever published. The monetary gains can also be a two-edged sword if one is astute with what the real world is about. Not all that glitters and is gold makes one happy.

In conclusion, I offer this work mainly for those who might believe that there are realities beyond what is considered normal and are willing to explore those thoughts. I offer this to those who may be helped by finding resonance with the words, whatever the source. I hold it up as a resource that may help some to find their giving natures, some to find the help they seek from others, and a reminder to envision a better world and to contribute as each one can. I have given it in the hopes that something in here that will shed light on the events of the accident. It is given in the spirit of truth from myself to all who have finished it. I also wish to let it stand as an effort of thanks to my guides who have helped me with many things in my world with their wisdom from their world. But most importantly,

I offer this because I was asked to do so by a very thoughtful and thought-provoking lady who came to me and made me feel wonderful things about our world, her current reality, and even myself. It is for the one whom I found that I could not deny the fulfillment of her request. This is my tribute to that great woman, Diana, a graceful and caring princess in any world.

CHAPTER 22

The Princess Bids Farewell

**** "These are my words for the closing of the book. When I was young, I had no idea that I would one day be the fairy-tale princess. It was not something that I seriously dreamed of until the day that Charles gave the inclination that he would consider me for this position. I was able to see that if I lived out the fairy tale to exacting standards that I would become the one who had gone from rags to riches in a metaphorical way. Not that I was ever in the realm of poverty, as so many are, but that if one as shy and gawky as I could become the princess of Wales, then anyone could have anything that they had yet to dream of.

"I was working on making the fairy tale more believable to me when I was taken from that world. It was a given that I wanted to impact the world for the better and was working at doing so. I would have been given the gift of seeing some of my dreams fulfilled had I lived a very long time there, but I have now ascertained that I can see all of them fulfilled if I so choose by working from this realm. There is a given that I can make no impact upon that world directly since I am no longer of physical substance enough to do so. However, the spirit that resided in that physical form that used to find ways to keep itself in shape is still intact and willing to work even harder to keep the dream of a universal world that allows no injustice, suffering, and ridicule of the less fortunate within its boundaries.

"I am remarkably able to see the future if such things begin to reach a critical mass of giving that I have a hard time not openly weeping with joy in my soul for this work to be done. I was once a dreamer of a better world, but now I am a seer of that world if the world would but find their own vision of this possibility. I would urge all to take heed of the words of this princess and allow the world to use what is its inherent birthright to be made the kingdom of God upon a physical world. There are many ways that I could explain the joy. The most colorful one is that when the earth reaches that critical mass situation, then all of the stars in the heavens will bow to the beauty of the light that is reflected from the earth's surface by those who glow with the light of God's love and wisdom. It is a beautiful light to see, and this is what I want for my children, the world that I loved, and the realms of spirit. There would be a giving to the realm of spirit yet another joy that cannot be imagined when you have but only bodies with which to feel.

"I have chosen to come forward and address the world through the use of this woman for she knows well what the world of spirit is about. She has chosen to use her own gifts to help those here work with your world, and I have found no other who can work as well with me or this world. I am well pleased with our joint effort and would ask that all who read my words should seek to have the same faith in the world of spirit that this one has shown. Her availability to me has been gracious and often wrought from a hectic schedule. It is with sincerest gratitude that I say thank you to her and to her friends who have helped maintain her spirit with this work. I would also like to thank those who have received me also, but do not yet know the validity that they have in this book. I can only ask that when you have encountered the faith of this one who steps forward that you work alongside of her for the combining of your wisdom of my words with that which she has and will have for the future.

"There is great spirit in teamwork, and I am requesting that all who want a better world work as a team with those who can and do hear me. It is the last request of the fairy-tale princess of those who showed such love and respect for her physical form. If there was a loving feeling for my form, then there must be a showing for the love of my spirit. I have often brimmed with joy over how well I was received when I was there, and I would once again like to feel that feeling of acceptance with my words and intentions from my present world. If there was love towards others as was shown to me, then the world would have reached a critical mass situation the first time I had appeared publicly, and the world greeted me with such warmth. This is my last request of that world. Love others as I had seen them try to love me, to work with great spirit of teamwork to make that better vision, and to allow those who can lead with great spirit and love know that this is what the world wants and will strive for.

"This is the goal of my attempt with this work. To create the ideal world for all and for the beginning of my son's reign. He will prove to be a just and fair man with much compassion and tolerance of others. He will assume the leadership of the world of the United Kingdom with great grace and dignity and will prove himself far greater than either of his parents for being able to maintain a sense of world spirit and attitude of giving to those who are his subjects. He has been taught well at the hands of many, and this is a source of pride for me that I was able to give him what I intended before I left that world. He will know that I have spoken for he knows that to work at being king means to work at being the protector and the way-shower for those who are under his care, and to set an example for the others who are rulers in the world. This is what I have tried to teach him, and he has learned well the value of being attuned to the common man's plight. He will grace the history books with uncommon wisdom and spirit of love for his subjects. It is not only a mother's bragging, but also what I have come to know of the future. It will be as if there had never been a fairy-tale princess once he is seated upon the throne for he will greatly eclipse anything that I had even hoped to do as the one who was fortunate to be married to a future king. His is a great destiny, and I am always his ever-loving mother in thought and deed.

"His brother will also ascend to greatness in his own right. He will become the one to offer wise counsel to his brother on issues that are of

his own soul's wisdom and they will make a for-
midable team for the reformation of a world not
yet seen since times not remembered or recorded.
I have seen the future of each, and I am extremely
proud to have been the vessel through which each
of these magnificent souls has made their entry
to the world of form. My work of greatest value
had been to be their mother and to have some
time with them. For this I am eternally blessed.
The right to work with them for this future was
indeed an honored assignment.

"There will be many who will scoff at the
words contained in these pages, but these are the
ones who fear the change the most. Those who
want this change and are knowing internally that
what I say is of being the future, will step forward
and embrace the gifts awaiting them to help with
this reformation. They will have no doubt and
no fear associated with the gift of these words of
mine. They will be the ones who change themselves to help change the world. To these brave
and valiant souls, I am deeply grateful and honored to have been the fairy-tale princess to make
the mark upon the world that I did, and that I
will. May we all find a place within us that can
harbor the gifts of spirit that are our birthright
irregardless of our place of birth or our position
of birth within the world as we once knew it to
be. We are the way of the future and we are the
ones who can affect those who are afraid. There
is no greater persuasion than seeing someone else
change and seeing the glory to which they are
taken when this change is wrought. These are the
words of the fairy-tale princess to those who follow the lead of their inner spirit and knowing
about my life and my soul.

"What was once derision and ridicule will become assistance and compassion. What was once a turning away from will become an embracing. The ones who will seek will find. All who find will work for the greater of the whole until no one is left to seek and all have been found. These are the words of the fairy-tale princess to the words of those who scoff. When the light is given with great force to all who have sought it, then the ones who have scoffed will make the change, for to not do so will make them more uncomfortable than they had ever been made uncomfortable with their old viewpoints held firmly in their grasp.

"It is for this purpose that I have come forward and my voice on your world has come forward. There can be no change until someone leads the way, and I have chosen to do so for my kingdom, my world that I inhabit now, my children, and the world that can be woven when someone gives a pattern to follow. With this pattern made up of all who can dream and can work towards their dreams of a better world, the tapestry will be world-encompassing, highly creative, and big enough to keep all warm and cozy when the winds blow cold.

"I have now considered myself a seamstress of the highest order and remember well my lessons of how not to prick your fingers. The pricking of my fingers while upon your world has taught me well that to prick one's finger is the only way to learn that care must be taken when weaving the frock that you truly desire. The frock will be just as lovely if you learn not to prick your finger upon vanity, wastefulness, excess, and indulgence in self-pity. There are other ways to prick your fingers, and each must learn their own techniques of how to avoid the pitfall of the wayward needle, but all will do so as they work upon their portion of this frock for the world.

"I am now well satisfied that I have made my comments clear and accurately enough that all may know that I can be found working upon your world from my own world. There is no doubt within those who truly knew my ways of thinking. There is no doubt within the one whom has chosen to be the fingers to write my words of love and care for that world. There will be no doubt as the world changes and the world sees the truth of my statements coming to fruition. There will be no doubt from those who have also spoken to me once they have the lead of these words from my assistant upon your world. Those who have doubt will need to look hard within themselves to where this fear comes from and why they resist so thoroughly the words that have been given from this world to that one.

"As each gaze into their own reflection, may they see the light of their own soul reflected back to them to soothe their fears and their doubts. The soul will lead if you will only follow. It was also a lesson that I could have used when I walked among those of your world. This is what I leave you with for the weaving of that beautiful party frock that will enhance the beauty of the world that you now live in. May God and grace be your light to undo the darkness of fear."

Diana

REFERENCES

Morton, Andrew. 1992. *Diana: Her True Story*. New York: Simon & Schuster.
The Holy Bible, King James Version.

RECOMMENDED RESEARCH

Websites

DianaSpeaks.info

Andrew Russell-Davis is also a channel for Diana. (She has always said to me she would use more than one voice!) He is a direct voice channel so Diana speaks using his vocal cords. He is the man mentioned in Diana's statements to me.

angelfire.com/mb2/diana_speaks/

Marcia McMahon's site covering Diana's more recent channelings to us for the world peace effort. A serious collection of words as given by Diana.

thestarsstillshine.com/dioct03.html

Robert Murray, who also channels and has spoken to Princess Diana, offers us her words. After reading these words, be sure to go to his home page to check out the rest of his site.

sessionswithspirit.info

Rose Campbell's personal website.

Books

With Love from Diana, Queen of Hearts by Marcia McMahon
Opening to Channel: How to Connect with Your Guide by Sanaya
    Roman and Duane Packer
Understanding Your Angels and Meeting Your Guides by John Edward
    Seth Speaks/The Nature of Personal Reality/The Seth Material by
Jane Roberts
Conversations with God series by Neale Donald Walsch
The Edgar Cayce books by various authors
Ask and It Is Given by Esther Hicks and the wise group of entities
    known as Abraham.
The Stars Still Shine: An Afterlife Journey by Robert Murray